Windows

assistant

CW00361598

BY THE SAME AUTHOR

Windows 98 assistant

by

Ian Sinclair

BERNARD BABANI (publishing) LTD
THE GRAMPIANS
SHEPHERDS BUSH ROAD
LONDON W6 7NF
ENGLAND

PLEASE NOTE

Although every care has been taken with the production of this book to ensure that any projects, designs, modifications and/or programs, etc., contained herewith, operate in a correct and safe manner and also that any components specified are normally available in Great Britain, the Publishers and Author(s) do not accept responsibility in any way for the failure (including fault in design) of any project, design, modification or program to work correctly or to cause damage to any equipment that it may be connected to or used in conjunction with, or in respect of any other damage or injury that may be so caused, nor do the Publishers accept responsibility in any way for the failure to obtain specified components.

Notice is also given that if equipment that is still under warranty is modified in any way or used or connected with home-built equipment then that warranty may be void.

© 1998 BERNARD BABANI (publishing) LTD

First Published – July 1998

British Library Cataloguing in Publication Data:

A catalogue record for this book is available from the British Library

ISBN 0 85934 454 1

Cover Design by Gregor Arthur

Cover Illustration by Adam Willis

Printed and Bound in Great Britain by Cox & Wyman Ltd, Reading

ABOUT THIS BOOK

The Windows 98 assistant is a new concept, a way of getting help whether you have the computer switched on or not. It's faster than clicking from one topic to another, and for most actions, you could have looked up your help in this book before the hard drive stops clicking on your computer on a similar mission. It has been written around Windows 98 and much of the advice will apply to later versions. Since Windows 98 incorporates Internet Explorer, the use of this browser is covered, as also is Outlook Express for Mail and News.

What makes this book different is its organisation. There is a short index of actions that are not listed in the main section, so that you can look up their use in the longer references. The main text consists of the most frequently needed aspects of Windows for which assistance is needed, all in alphabetical order. In this list, even the main menu items of Windows (like Start) have entries so that you can remind yourself of the most elementary points as well as of the details of actions that may be new to you, along with advice and notes that you may not have thought of. In all cases, you should look up the main word in any phrase. For example, if you want to look up *documents list*, the important word is *document* and that's what you look up in the main index.

In addition, there are notes and comments so that you can see why one method might be preferable to another, or why you might want to use some Windows 98 command that you have no experience with.

To make this book useful without being too bulky, some complications have been omitted. We assume that you *use* Windows 98 as distinct from being a programmer who is writing for Windows, so that topics like Visual Basic or macros are omitted. We assume that you want Help with Windows, not for Word, Excel or Access. We assume that you are working solo or in a small network, and that someone else can organise actions like Internet connection and setting up email.

What we have done is to concentrate on the assistance that is most needed. In each item dealt with, the sub-headings are not necessarily in alphabetical order, because that's not the order in which you need help. The main part of this book provides your assistance, and there is also an index of cross-references at the start of the book so that you can look up terms that are not included in the main index.

Take a look, try it for yourself. At a time when manufacturers have abandoned manuals in favour of Help files, real help is here, at hand.

NOTE: Windows 98 allows you to choose whether to work in the older way with a double-click to start a program running or open a document, or to work using a single click for these actions. You are reminded by underlined file names when the single-click system is being used. Throughout this book, I have assumed that you have opted for the later single-click system.

Ian Sinclair, Spring 1998

ABOUT THE AUTHOR

Ian Sinclair was born in 1932 in Tayport, Fife, and graduated from the University of St. Andrews in 1956. In that year, he joined the English Electric Valve Co. in Chelmsford, Essex, to work on the design of specialised cathode-ray tubes, and later on small transmitting valves and TV transmitting tubes.

In 1966, he became an assistant lecturer at Hornchurch Technical College, and in 1967 joined the staff of Braintree College of F.E. as a lecturer. His first book, "Understanding Electronic Components" was published in 1972, and he has been writing ever since, particularly for the novice in Electronics or Computing. The interest in computing arose after seeing a Tandy TRS80 in San Francisco in 1977, and of his 180 published books, about half have been on computing topics, starting with a guide to Microsoft Basic on the TRS80 in 1979.

He left teaching in 1984 to concentrate entirely on writing, and has also gained experience in computer typesetting, particularly for mathematical texts. He has recently visited Seattle to see Microsoft at work, and to remind them that he has been using Microsoft products longer than most Microsoft employees can remember.

ACKNOWLEDGEMENTS

I would like to thank the staff of Text 100 Ltd. for providing the Windows 98 software on which this book has been based. I am also grateful to Microsoft for answers to my questions, and to many individuals who corresponded through News groups.

TRADEMARKS

PREFACE

Windows 98 has evolved rather than appearing suddenly, and anyone who bought a new computer in 1997/1998 and installed Internet Explorer 4 in addition to the Windows 95 version will already be familiar with the appearance of Windows 98. If, on the other hand, you bought your computer in 1995/1996 and use Internet Explorer 3, the changes that you will see in Windows 98 will be considerable.

Windows 98 now contains Internet access as a part of the operating system rather than as an add-on, and parts of the operating system such as Windows Explorer now look almost indistinguishable from the Internet Explorer. This integration means that applications running under Windows 98 now have the same sort of access to Internet files as the older version had to internal (local) files, and the appearance of Windows 98 is much closer to that of Internet Explorer than to Windows 95.

If you bought a computer equipped with the later version (OSR2 or FAT32) of Windows 95, and you have no interest in Internet use, you might consider that you had no particular reason for changing to Windows 98. This is not so, because Windows 98 contains a large number of changes that add up to provide faster and more efficient handling, and a considerable number of additions that help you to overcome difficulties.

Actions have also changed, with greater use of single-click actions, better access to driver files, faster booting and shutting down, a new Backup system that can use a wider variety of devices, and a new set of maintenance and diagnostic utilities.

In the past, a separate Assistant book was used for Internet Explorer 3, but in this book, the Internet aspects of Windows 98 have been dealt with under their respective headings so that no separate volume is needed.

Cross-reference Index

Add hardware, *see* Hardware

Add programs, see Add/remove programs

Applications, see Add/remove programs, Explorer, Start button

Automatic backup, *see* Backup

Background, *see* Desktop

Bulletin boards, *see* Hyperterminal

Calibrating display, *see* Display

Clearing documents, *see* Documents

Click speed, *see* Mouse

Closing window, *see* Window

Closing program, *see* Window

Context-sensitive menus, *see* Right-hand mouse button

Copying files, *see* Explorer

Cutting and pasting, *see* Copying objects

Date, *see* Country (regional) settings, Date/time

Decimal format *see* Country (regional) settings

Deleted files *see* Recycle Bin

Dialler directories, *see* Dialler

Disassociating file types, *see* Associating files

Drive letters, *see* My Computer

Drivers, *see* Hardware

Drivespace, *see* Compressed drives

Drop drawings, *see* Drag and drop

Dump screen, *see* Printing

Embedding, *see* Objects

Extended characters, *see* Character Map

32-bit PC card

General: This option is useful only if your computer has a PCMCIA card socket installed. This is more likely to be present if you are using a laptop machine or if your desktop PC has to provide for reading PCMCIA cards from laptop machines.

Enabling: If the computer had a PCMCIA socket connected before installing Windows 98, then the controller software will have been installed. If not, you can click Start — Help — 32-bit PC Card Support to get to the *To enable32-bit PC card support* item. This contains a <u>Click here</u> hyperlink that will start the installation wizard.

Disabling: Start Control Panel and click *System* to bring up *Device Manager*. If you have a 32-bit card socket, you will see the item *PC /Card Slot* and you can click the [+] sign to find *PCMCIA controller*. Double-click on this, and click to remove the tick from *Disable in this hardware profile* box in *Device Usage*. You should also modify the three text files called Config.sys, Autoexec.bat and System.ini to remove the line that reads:

REM - by PC Card (PCMCIA) wizard

You should then save the files, close them and restart the computer.

---

3 D graphics and ActiveX

General: 3-D graphics look very pretty, but like all images transmitted over the Internet they take up a lot of space and need time to load over the telephone lines. ActiveX controls are buttons and other objects that can be used as hypertext links. The use of Active-X means that you can view a document using Explorer without the need to start the application that created the document.

Use: 3-D graphics are used mainly as buttons to click for (hyper)links to another document or other material. When a 3-D image is a hyperlink, the mouse pointer will change to the shape of a hand when placed over the image.

Options: You can use View — Options to turn off the *Show pictures* option, which will stop some types of picture from appearing, leaving hyperlinks visible as words or simple images. For maximum speed you can turn off *Play sounds* and *Play videos* as well.

Active-X: Programming with ActiveX is for skilled users only, and beyond the scope of this book.

Accelerator keys

General: Internet Explorer allows you full use with the mouse, but you can often save time by using key actions. Some of these keys and key combinations are instinctive, others need to be learned if you are to use them often. The following list contains all the common key/combinations, and you might find several of these useful.

Action	Key(s)
Next page	Shift-Backspace
Previous page	Backspace
Shortcut menu for a hyperlink	Shift-F10
Move between frames	Shift-Ctrl-Tab
Scroll by 2-lines to start	↑
Scroll by 2 lines to end	↓

Action	Key(s)
Scroll by one page to start	PgUp
Scroll by one page to end	PgDn
Move to start	Home
Move to end	End
Refresh current page	F5
Stop downloading a page	Esc
Go to a new location	Ctrl-O
Open a new window	Ctrl-N
Save the current page	Ctrl-S
Print the current page or active frame	Ctrl-P
Activate a selected hyperlink	ENTER

Access, Internet

General: Access to the Internet is normally made by connection through telephone lines to a computer belonging to an information provider (IP). You will be charged for this service, and charges vary widely; some are based on time of usage, others on a flat rate. You should spend some time assessing the different rates before making a decision — remember that if you later change IPs, you may have to notify all of your contacts on e-mail that you have a different e-mail address. You should tell your IP that you are using Windows 98. If you are using a new modem to the V90 standard (56K) you should also check that your IP can connect at this speed. For business purposes, the ISDN type of permanent connection is more useful than a modem connection.

Windows 98 assistant

Connection: Check that your modem is correctly installed and is connected to the telephone point. Your IP will provide software on a CD-ROM. Run this to load software and make the connection.

- Some IPs in the USA can be contacted direct from Windows 98. These will always include MSN and you can also find AOL in this set.

Adjustments: Some IP's software will make all the adjustments that you need; others will need further tweaks. Make sure that your password is memorised, otherwise you will have to type it in each time you make connection. Most of the adjustments you may have to make are dealt with in the *Dial Up Networking* folder, see the entry for this item.

Accessibility

General: Windows 98 contains a set of options that are intended to help users who find difficulties with using the default screen, mouse, sound, or keyboard systems. Some of these options, such as the sound effects when the Caps Lock key is pressed, are also useful to other users.

Selecting options: Use Start — Settings — Control Panel and when the Control Panel appears, click on *Accessibility Options*. This brings up a set of five panels, each with several items that can be switched on or off by clicking on a box, and each with a *Settings* button that allows you to customise the settings.

Keyboard: You can opt for *Sticky Keys* for one-finger typing, so that the Shift, Ctrl, and Alt keys can be used immediately ahead of a letter key rather than by pressing both together. The *FilterKeys* option can be turned on so that the machine will ignore either a key that is briefly stabbed or that is pressed several times in rapid succession. The

ToggleKey action will provide a sound warning when any of the lock keys is used (Caps lock, Num lock or Scroll lock). One sound indicates that a lock key has been switched on, another sound indicates that the lock has been switched off.

Sound: *SoundSentry* will provide a visual warning when a sound is used. *ShowSound* will display a caption for speech or sound effects.

Display: You can opt for colours and fonts for easier viewing by clicking the *Use High Contrast* box. The *Settings* button allows you to select the type of scheme, and assign a shortcut key.

Mouse: You can opt for *Use MouseKeys*, using the cursor keys on the numeric keypad instead. The *Settings* button provides a shortcut key, and the control of pointer speed, acceleration, status display, and use with Numlock.

General: The *AutoReset* option provides for turning off all accessibility commands after a fixed time, such as 5 minutes. *Notification* provides options for issuing warning sounds when features are turned on or off. Finally, you can opt for using *SerialKey* devices if you have such a (hardware) item connected.

Notes: You should try out some of these actions to find if they would be useful to you. The sound warning about pressing the Caps Lock key is particularly useful.

Active content

General: Active content, referring to Internet downloads, means animated displays, multimedia shows and other displays or actions that require a program to be downloaded from the Internet and run. Since this poses a security risk (the program could introduce a virus) you need to specify that you want such active content files.

Windows 98 assistant

Selecting: Click on the *View* menu of Internet Explorer, and then on Internet Options — Security. For the material labelled as Internet Zone, select the security rating (High, Medium, Low or Custom) that you want to use. For most purposes, the *Medium* setting is a good compromise. The *High* setting provides the maximum security, but can make it impossible to read some pages simply because they contain program material. A *Medium* setting warns you about such material, and allows you to decide for yourself if the supplier is trustworthy.

For Internet sites that you place in the *Trusted sites zone* the security level is normally set to *Low*. Do not use *Custom* unless you are knowledgeable about security risks.

Add/remove programs

General: When Windows 98 was installed on your computer, it will have installed the same options as you used for Windows 95, and your version may contain programs that you never intend to use. You can remove these unwanted files and, equally important, restore them or add others as needed, if you follow the procedure illustrated here. Programs other than the Windows 98 set can also be added or removed using the same methods.

Note that Windows 98 also contains the **Disk Cleanup** utility to remove programs, see under this heading.

Uninstalling W'98 files: Start Control Panel, either from Explorer or from Start — Settings. click on *Add/Remove Programs* and when the panel appears click the *Windows Setup* tab. You will see a list of the sections of Windows that can be altered. These main headings are:

Accessibility   Accessories   Communications

Desktop Themes	Internet Tools	Microsoft Outlook Express
Multilanguage Support	Multimedia	Online Services
System Tools	Web TV for Windows	

There is a small selection box at each title, blank if nothing in that section is used, ticked if all of the section is used. If only a selection of files is used, the box will be shaded grey and ticked. You can either add or remove a tick, or you can click the *Details* button to alter the selection of actions within a section. Click the *OK* button when you have completed your selection of details or your choices of main sections. If you are only removing files, you do not normally need to have the original CD-ROM or floppy discs present, but if your selection involves adding a new file, you must have the original source disc(s) in the appropriate drive and use the *Have Disk* button.

Installing W98 files: Follow the procedure noted above, adding ticks to sections and sub-sections of the list. Make sure that the distribution CD-ROM is in its drive before you finally click on the OK button to start installation. If you are using a floppy disc set, you will be asked to insert various discs.

Other Programs: Start *Add/Remove Programs* as above from Control Panel, and use the *Install/Uninstall* tab. To uninstall a program that is shown on the list, select it and click the *Add/Remove* button. You will be asked to confirm that you want to remove the program. To install a program, you must have a source disc, either a floppy (the first of a set) or a CD-ROM in the appropriate drive. Click the *Install* button so that Windows will search for a program called

Windows 98 assistant

Install or *Setup* on the distribution disc. Once this is found, you can click to start the installation process.

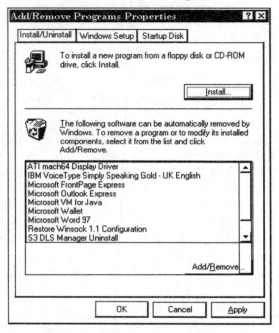

Notes: You should use **only** this system for adding or removing **Windows** files. If you remove parts of the Windows system by deleting from the Explorer view, there is a risk that you will remove files that cannot be restored by way of the *Setup* action, and you will then need to restore using the MS-DOS EXTRACT command (see the entry in this book). You can remove older programs by deleting their files, but if the name of a program appears on the *Uninstall* list it is always better to use this method of removing it.

If you have removed programs, but you find that their names still appear in the *Uninstall* list, this is because the registry entry still exists. You can use a separate uninstaller program to remove these remnants and this is preferable to altering the registry.

Address bar

General: the address bar of Internet Explorer is used by default to show the full address of the current page or a page that is being downloaded. You can turn this facility off if you do not need it.

Changing address bar: Click on View — Toolbars and click on the *Address bar* box. With the Address bar visible, you can click on the left hand side (at the vertical bar) and drag the bar around to reduce its size. All toolbars can be altered in this way.

Links: The first time you visit a Web site you will either need to click on the address in a list on the home page, or type it for yourself. You can speed up this action in subsequent visits by specifying that links appear on the Toolbar. Click View — Toolbars and make sure that the *Links* box in the Toolbar section is ticked. You can drag an address to this Toolbar and drop it between existing links.

Other options: If you need to use a new Web address, you can click File — New Window before typing the address so that the new material is not laid over the old pages. Some Web pages will automatically open a new window for you. You can also go to a new address by using File — Open and then typing the address in the *Open* space. You can use the *Browse* button in this panel to look for addresses that have been saved as files.

ASCII files

General: ASCII files (also called plain text files) can be read by any software that handles text, and are essential for editing some types of files of commands, such as AUTOEXEC.BAT or CONFIG.SYS, and for specialised purposes, such as saving or editing an exclusion dictionary for Word. In addition, an ASCII file takes up much less disc space than a formatted word-processor file and less than an Internet HTML file. ASCII files consist of codes for the letters and punctuation marks of the alphabet, plus the numbers 0 to 9, but they are unformatted (with no fonts, bold, italics, underline or other effects).

Creating: Use the *Notepad* utility of Windows 98 to type or edit text which will be saved as an ASCII file. Notepad is limited to files of less than 64K characters, corresponding to about 8,000 words. For longer ASCII files, use the *WordPad* utility with the *Save As* option of *Text Document – MS-DOS Format* rather than the default of *Word for Windows*. The older *Write* utility (part of Windows 3.1) can also save files in ASCII form (called *Text files*).

Notes: Use ASCII format to store **archive** text (text for long-term backup), since this allows you to store more of your text in a limited space. See also the entries in this book for **Notepad** and **WordPad**.

If you click on a text file in Explorer, it will usually appear loaded in Notepad (or optionally in WordPad for a long file).

Associating files

General: A data file and a program can be associated, meaning that you can click a data file and so run the associated program with the data file loaded. For example, if any file with the TXT extension is associated with Notepad, then clicking a TXT file will have the effect of starting Notepad with the TXT file loaded for editing or reading.

Several associations (such as TXT with Notepad) are already made for you when you install Windows 98.

Checking and creating: If you have a data file that you want to use, simply open the Explorer window to find the file and click on the filename. If the file already has an association made, the appropriate program will start and load the file. If no association has been made for this file type, you will see the *Open with* panel appear. You can type a brief description of the file (such as *AutoSketch drawing*), and then select a program from the list that appears. The option of *Always use this program to open this file* is ticked by default, so that clicking any file with the same extension letters will, in future, cause the same program to start. Click on the *OK* button when you have selected a file, but if you do not see the appropriate program in the list, click the *Other* button to see a full list of all programs on your disc.

Changing association: View your files using Explorer or My Computer. Click the *View* menu and then *Folder options*. When the *Options* panel appears, click the *File

Types tab to see the list of programs for which associations exist. Click on the file type whose association you want to change – you will be reminded of the current settings in the *File Type Details* box. Click the *Edit* button. You can now alter the association. You must delete the current association before you assign a new one. A program can be associated with several file types, but a file type can be associated with only one program.

The *Change Icon* button allows you to select another icon (for the data file) from a list. You can also alter the *Description of Type* text. The *Actions* box contains a list of actions that can be used on the data file, usually *open* and *print*. Click on *Open* and then click the *Edit* button. Click the *Browse* button to see a tree of all folders and files so that you can select the program that you want to associate with this data file type.

Options: The *New* button on the *Edit Association* panel allows you to specify another action (other than the default *open* and *print*). You need to know what actions are possible and these depend on the type of file you are associating. The *Remove* button allows you to remove an association, so that clicking the data filename will not automatically start a program (though you will see the *Association* panel inviting you to select a suitable program).

You can also click the option boxes labelled *Enable QuickView*, *Always show extension*, *Confirm open after download* and (where applicable) *Browse in same window*.

Notes: Association is possible only if you have a suitable program on your hard drive, so that if you have imported a file from another computer you may not be able to associate it with any program on your own hard drive. See also the entry for **File types**.

Attributes of files

General: All files can be 'marked' with codes that are used to allow Windows 98 and MS-DOS to distinguish the files as belonging to four classes, and these codes are called *attributes*. A file can have no attributes, or any combination of the four. The four main file attributes are named *archive*, *hidden*, *read-only* and *system*, and of these the *archive* and *read-only* may sometimes need to be altered. The system and hidden attributes are set on for important files and should never be altered. Setting a file as *read-only* prevents editing, and the file can only be viewed, copied, or printed until this attribute is switched off. Setting a file as *archive* allows it to be backed up by any utility that recognises this attribute – the archive code is set when a file has been altered since the last time it was backed up and reset (switched off) when a backup is made.

Change attributes: Use an *Explorer* or *My Computer* display to find the file, and click the filename. Now click *File* and *Properties* from the menu. The attributes appear as a set of four boxes at the bottom of the *Properties* panel. Usually the archive box is ticked but the others are not – the system attribute box is usually greyed out. You would normally want to use this action to set a file as read-only or to clear the read-only attribute to allow editing.

Notes: Some programs (such as Word) allow you to set the read-only attribute directly for a file. The archive bits are sometimes referred to as R–A–S–H, using the initial letters of read-only, archive, system and hidden.

- You can opt to see, in an Explorer display, files that are normally hidden. See the entry for **System files**.

- The archive attribute is not reset when you make a copy to a floppy, only when a backup system is used, such as Backup in Windows, or XCOPY in MS-DOS.

Autoexec.bat file

General: The AUTOEXEC.BAT file consists of an ASCII text file containing a set of MS-DOS commands that are executed before Windows 98 is loaded, and you should not, in normal circumstances, need to edit this file. Its purpose is to set up the computer, particularly for running MS-DOS programs or for additions (such as sound cards) that were installed before Windows 98. If your computer was in use before Windows 95/98 was installed (using Windows 3.1 or even DOS) then several portions of the file will have been modified by the installation program for Windows 98.

Editing: Start Notepad and use the *Open* command to look for *All files* (*.*). Look in the C:\ root folder and click AUTOEXEC.BAT. The file can then be edited. See *BP341 MS-DOS 6 explained* for details of how to use this file.

Bypassing: If a command in the AUTOEXEC.BAT file is causing problems with Windows 98, you can start the computer in such a way as to bypass these commands. Restart the computer by using Start — Shut Down, and hold down the **left** Ctrl key while the machine starts. **On some machines you need to hold down the F8 key rather than the Ctrl key — find out which applies to your machine**.

Note that if Windows starts and you then restart your computer, the Scandisk program will run automatically the next time you start Windows.

From the menu that appears, select *Step by Step Confirmation*. This allows you to accept or reject each step in the setup, starting with the commands of the

CONFIG.SYS file (see entry for **CONFIG.SYS**). The final step should be the AUTOEXEC.BAT file (or *Startup Command File*, as it is referred to). If you do not use this file, you can avoid starting Windows 98 and the machine will be running DOS.

Notes: If you have never used DOS, and particularly if your computer was installed with Windows 98 when you bought it, you should never need to edit AUTOEXEC.BAT or CONFIG.SYS, and you should certainly not do so unless you understand the effects that changes in these files could cause.

Available disc space

General: If you have a large hard drive (more than 2.0 Gbyte) which is less than half filled, you hardly need worry about disc space. If, however, you are using a hard drive of inadequate size then you need to check available disc space at intervals. You may also want to check the available space on a floppy disc.

Methods: The simplest check is available in the *Explorer* window when the drive (hard or floppy) is selected. The available disc space is printed at the foot of the *Explorer* window, along with the space taken up by files in the selected folder.

Another option is to use *My Computer*, click the drive icon for the drive, and then click File — Properties. This brings up a pie chart which will show the relative sizes of used and unused space. You can also use Explorer, right-click the drive and click on *Properties*.

Notes: Older drives may have used the *DriveSpace* compression system to allow more to be packed on to a drive. The falling prices of large hard drives have made this system obsolete. Windows 98 uses a revised disc system that makes any such compression unnecessary, and which also uses large hard drives more efficiently. See entry for **Drive Converter**.

Backup

General: Backup will make a compressed copy of selected files, folders or a complete drive to any suitable storage medium. You can also use Backup to compare a backed-up file with the original, and to retrieve files from backed-up form. The process is automatic once started, though if you use floppies for saving large amounts of data you will need to change discs at intervals — about 4 Mbyte can be saved on each floppy. Windows 98 recognises a wide range of backup systems, unlike W95, and the recognised manufacturers are AIWA, APS, Active, Combyte, Compaq, Conner, Exabyte, Fujitsu, HP/Colorado, IBM, Iomega, MicroSolutions, Mountain, Pertec, Rexon, Seagate, Sony, Tandberg, Teac, Tecmon, TTI and Wangtek. You can back up to local, removable or network drives.

- At the time of writing, not all backup systems had been tested by Seagate, but the only drive that is listed as incompatible is the Ditto 3-Gbyte, though there is doubt over the T4000s from Hewlett-Packard CMS.

- Note that if you use Seagate Backup 2.0 it must be removed if you want to use the Backup of Windows 98.

Starting: Click the *Start* button, followed by *Programs*, *Accessories* and *System Tools*. From the *System Tools* set, click *Backup*. The main *Microsoft Backup* wizard panel will appear. This provides the initial choice of *Create a new backup job*, *Open an existing backup job*, and *Restore backed up files*.

New backup job: When you use this option you will be asked to opt for *Back up My Computer*, meaning all files and folders on your hard drive(s), or to back up selected files, folders or drives. The option to back up everything is useful only if you are using a tape drive with adequate capacity, though if your tape cartridges are of lower capacity than your hard drive the backup can still be carried out by replacing the cartridge when asked.

The option to backup a selection will show you an Explorer view of your folders and files, with a small box next to each name. Click this box to place a tick into it and so select it. Selecting a drive will select all folders and files on that drive. Selecting a folder name will select for backup all the files in that folder. You can also select filenames individually. If a large number of files is selected the process can take several minutes.

Making the backup: When files have been selected, you can click the *Next* button. This allows you to backup all of the selected files or only the files that have changed (or are new) since the previous backup. Note that this option can considerably reduce the use of tape, because if you have made a full backup at some stage you do not need to do so again.

The next step is to select a destination for the backup, and if you do not have a tape drive, the selected option is *File*. This file can be placed on a hard or a floppy drive or on a network drive. If you have a tape drive, this can be selected as a QIC80 device. You will be asked for a name for the backup job, so that the same action can be repeated if needed.

If you are backing up to a floppy, note that the compression allows around 4.5 Mbyte to be stored on each floppy, and you will be asked to change disc at intervals if needed. If you have opted for the default verification, you will be asked to insert the floppies into the drive again, in the correct order.

File set: If you are likely to back up the same selection several times, you can make use of the name that you have used for the backup job. This is particularly useful if you have selected several folders, because if the contents of the folders change, they will still be automatically selected for backup because the folder has been selected.

Full System Backup: The *Back up My Computer* option will backup all of the files on the hard drive, including the important Windows registry files, so that you should make at least one backup of this type if you have a tape drive or a removable hard drive (the size of the FSB makes it unlikely that you will want to use floppies for this purpose).

Options, backup: The Options button on the opening page of Backup allows you to specify options in a set of panes labelled *General*, *Password*, *Type*, *Exclude*, *Report* and *Advanced*.

The *General* set starts with the option of *Compare original and backup files to verify data was successfully backed up*, and this is ticked by default. For peace of mind, you should leave this switched on, but if you are totally convinced of the integrity of your backups you can click to remove the tick. The second set of options are for compression, with the default of maximising compression — the other options are not to compress or to compress for optimum saving of time. The last options box in this set deals with the use of media that already contain backups, and allow you to append data, overwrite, or (very usefully) to choose the option when the backup starts.

The *Password* pane allows you to opt to use a password, and to enter and then confirm the word you want to use, which is not displayed on the screen. You should not use a password

18

unless it is really necessary, because any password that you can easily remember is likely to be equally easy to guess.

Type refers to the type of backup, and the default is All selected files. If you opt for New and changed files only, you can choose between *Differential* backup or *Incremental* backup. *Differential* backup is slower, but with faster restore action, and *Incremental* is the reverse, faster backup and slower restore.

The *Exclude* pane allows you to make a list of file types that you want to exclude from backups, possibly because you don't need to back them up, or because you back them up separately. Click the *Add* button to see a list of file types that you can exclude by adding them into this list.

Report deals with the log that is kept for a backup. The items in this set are *List all files that were backed up*, *List files that were not backed up*, *List errors reported while backing up files*, *List warnings reported while backing up files*, *List unattended messages and prompts*, and *Show summary report*. There is also a box marked *Perform unattended backup*, and this can be ticked so that no messages or prompts appear while backing up.

The *Advanced* section has just one option, *Back up Windows Registry*, which is ticked by default. You should keep this option ticked so that the Registry will be backed up in any action that deals with the C:\WINDOWS folder.

Restore action: When you click the *Restore* tab, the *Restore from* box should list the device you are using for backup, File or QIC80 device. You may need to click the *Refresh* button to make the name of the backup job appear in the *Catalog* window.

You also have to specify in the *Where to restore* box whether you want to restore to the original locations or to other folders or drives. If you specify an alternate location, you will see another box open so that you can click and browse for a folder. The *How to restore* box will by default contain Do not replace unless you have changed the default option, see later.

Once these choices have been made, you can click the Start button to carry out the restoration action.

Restore options: The *Options* button in the *Restore* pane contains *General*, *Report* and *Advanced*. The *General* section deals with replacing files that already exist, and the default is not to replace such files. This avoids the possibility of replacing a perfectly good file with a backup copy that might be corrupted. The other options are to replace a file that is older, or always to replace the file.

The *Report* options are the same as for the *Backup* option, and the *Advanced* option is to restore the Windows Registry. This last option is one that should be ticked only if the Registry has been lost, because restoring the Registry from tape will inevitably restore an older copy, unless the backup was made a short time earlier. Use an older copy only if your current Registry is totally corrupted and cannot be restored in any other way.

Menus: The menu items of Backup and Restore are *Job*, *Edit*, *View*, *Tools* and Help. The *Job* options are *New*, *Open*, *Save*, *Save As*, *Delete* and *Options*, with *Recent File* usually greyed out, and *Exit*. Once you have selected a backup job, you can save the Job as a file using *Save As*, and treat this file of instructions as you would any other file. The older Backup of Windows 95 called this file a *File Set*.

The *Edit* menu consists of *Select Space* and *Deselect*, both usually greyed out, and *View* allows you the options of seeing the *Toolbar*, the *Status bar* and the *Job details*. You can choose *List* or *Details* for the job descriptions, and see the *Selection information* relating to files you have selected.

20

The *Refresh* item is used to ensure that file displays are updated.

The Tools menu contains Wizards for both *Backup* and *Restore* if you feel uncertain about using the processes directly, and the other items are *Media*, *Report* and *Preferences*. The *Media* set relates to tape drives only, and contains *Identify*, *Initialize*, *Format*, *Retension* and *Rename*. These options are seldom needed, though the ability to identify an unknown tape is useful, as is the action of renaming a tape.

The *Report* item allows you either to *View* or *Print* the report relating to a backup or restore action. The report does not show filenames and consists only of items such as *Job Name*, with date and time of starting and finishing. The *Preferences* are all ticked by default and consist of:

Show startup dialogue when Microsoft Backup is started
Back up or restore the registry when backing up or restoring the Windows directory (folder)
Show the number and size of files before backing up, restoring and comparing data.

Notes: Tape drives that operate via the parallel port may not appear in the Device Manager list.

The new Windows 98 Backup (written by Seagate) is able to read files that were created using the Windows 95 Backup (written by HP/Colorado), since the file format is the same QIC type. If you have been accustomed to using the older version you should take some time to learn the new system, which differs in many ways. In particular, you may find that it tries to restore files to the folders that existed in the computer that created the files, which is not very useful if you have subsequently changed to a new computer or have rearranged your folders. Use the *Restore Wizard*, specify *Alternate Locations*, and click to show your current folder set if you encounter this problem. The older Backup was simpler and faster in this respect.

Battery actions

General: Modern laptop computers are not noted for long battery life, and Windows 98 contains utilities that assist in monitoring the state of the battery and reducing the drain on the battery. Several such items are usually built into the hardware, such as running the hard drive only when necessary, dimming the display, and shutting off other actions when not in use. Some of these options are available for mains-powered desktop machines as well.

The battery extending actions in Windows 98 assume the use of modern hardware, such as Advanced Power Management (*APM 1.1*) or the VESA BIOS extensions for power management (*VBE/PM*). No battery-saving options will appear unless the hardware of your computer supports them.

- Remember that Nickel-Cadmium (NiCad) batteries should be totally discharged before recharging. If you use your portable extensively you should keep a charged spare set, and you may be able to obtain a charger/discharger that will ensure that a battery is discharged before discharging. Some later battery types do not need a discharge cycle.

Monitor: Click *Start*, followed by *Settings* and *Control Panel*, and from Control Panel click *Display*. Now select the *Screen Saver* tab. For suitable hardware, there will be a box labelled *Energy saving features of monitor* and a *Settings* button that you can click.

In the *Settings* pane, the first tab is called *Power schemes*, and the default scheme is always on, with options of

Home/Office desk and *Portable/Laptop*. Use the setting appropriate to your computer and how you use it. These settings will appear below, if your monitor supports them, so that the monitor will be switched off after a set time of inactivity — you can select this time, usually five or ten minutes, in the *System standby* box. The *Shut Off Monitor* box can also be ticked (specifying a longer time than the *Standby* period). You may find, depending on your monitor type, that your monitor settings can be altered from an icon in the Taskbar line

At the foot of the panel you will see a hard drive option labelled *Turn off hard discs* with a time that can be varied from 3 minutes to 5 hours or *Never*. This specifies what time can elapse before the hard drive motor is switched down to save energy.

Battery meter: If your hardware has been correctly installed, there will be an icon on the Taskbar for checking battery condition – this can be an image of a battery or a (US-type) electric plug. Point to this icon to find what percentage of a full charge is available to you, or click for more information on battery state. If no *Power* icon appears on the Taskbar, click the *Power Properties* icon in Control Panel – this will appear only if the hardware supports these features.

Notes: Use a car or mains adapter as far as is possible for supplying your portable so as to reduce the drain on the internal batteries. Try to download important data to home base as often as is possible. Nickel Cadmium batteries are notorious for their 'memory effect' — unless they are fully discharged, they will not charge fully, and users of camcorders can buy battery dischargers for this purpose.

Briefcase

General: Briefcase is a facility aimed at anyone who uses a portable machine working on files that are copied from a desktop machine in the office. With the machines connected (by direct cable or over a network), you can drag files from the main computer to the *Briefcase* icon on the portable computer, and use these files when the machines are disconnected. When you reconnect, clicking the option of *Update All in Briefcase* will automatically update all the affected files in the desktop computer so that they are identical to the altered version in the portable machine. Briefcase is available only if you selected the *Portable* option when Windows 98 was installed on the portable machine (or if you performed a *Custom* installation and specified *Briefcase*). If your portable machine does not show the Briefcase icon on its Desktop display, you can repeat the *Install* action to install just this one component.

Checking files: Using the *Briefcase* folder, click the file(s) you want to check. Click File — Properties and click the *Update Status* tab. If you are connected to the main computer, you can click *Find Original* to get the file whose copy is in the portable machine. You can check all of the *Briefcase* files (and folders) from the View — Details menu, reading the *Status* report for each file that appears.

Using a floppy: Files can be updated even if there is no cable or network connection between the desktop machine and the portable, but the set of actions is more complicated. The desktop machine must have used the *Portable* setup option so that the *My Briefcase* icon appears on the Desktop (use Setup if necessary to install this icon). With a floppy in the drive of the desktop machine, drag files/folders to the *My Briefcase* icon on the desktop. Drag the *Briefcase* to the floppy drive symbol to copy the files to the floppy. Remove the floppy from the desktop computer and insert it into the portable. Copy the files and edit them in the portable, copying back to the floppy when completed.

Back in the office, put the floppy into its drive in the desktop machine and click the *My Briefcase* icon on the desktop. Click the *Update All* item in the *Briefcase* menu. If you want to select files for updating, make the selection and click *Update Selection*.

Orphans: An orphan is a file that has been split from the original (on the main computer), so that it belongs entirely with the portable machine and cannot be used to update the corresponding file on the main machine (except by copying it to the main machine). To create an orphan, click the file and click the *Split from Original* menu item.

Notes: The *Briefcase* action is also referred to as *synchronising files*. See also **Direct cable connection** for linking computers by cable.

Browsing

General: Browsing is searching, either with a definite aim, or more generally looking for anything of interest, also called *surfing*. Internet Explorer makes it easier for either type of browsing.

Specific page: Type the full Internet address of the page that you want in the address box and press the RETURN or ENTER key. A Web address will normally start with http://www, and if slashmarks are used at the end of the address, this signifies that you are looking for sub-documents or specific pages or topics. Internet Explorer will allow you to omit the http:// part of an address. For Web addresses that you have used before in the same session, click the down-arrow at the right hand side of the address space to select from the list of addresses.

Searching: If Internet Explorer is not already running, click the Start — Find item on the menu — the options of *Files and Folders*, *Computer*, *On the Internet*, *On the Internet* and *People* will appear. The *Files and Folders* option is the same as the older Windows Explorer option of Windows 95. The *Computer* option applies only if you are working over a network, and *On the Internet* will make use of the Internet default search engine. The *People* option allows you to find another Internet user by specifying E-mail address or name. The default search engine for looking for people is *WhoWhere* at address http://www.whowhere.com/. You can also use your own *Address Book*, and the services of *Four11*, *Infospace*, *InfoSpace Business*, *SwitchBoard* or *Verisign*. To alter the search agent, click on the arrowhead at the side of the address bar.

Organising pages*:* With an Internet page in view, click *Favorites* on the Toolbar, and then click the *Add to favorites* item in this menu (you can select a sub-folder). See the entry for **Favourites** for more information.

Returning to a page: Click the left-facing arrow symbol to go back one page, and repeat as needed. You can also click the arrowhead next to the arrow to see a list of locations that you have viewed. Alternatively, click the *Go* menu, and look at the list of pages that you have used in the current session. Click on the page you want to return to. If you want to return to a page you have viewed in a previous session, click on *Open History folder* and select from the list that is displayed.

Stop button: The toolbar button that is marked with a cross is the *Stop* button, and you can use it to terminate a download that is taking too long. This may happen when you are contacting a U.S. computer in the late afternoon or evening, or when you are trying to get to a very busy site, or if you are trying to download a very large file.

Working offline: If you have previously downloaded Web pages, you can work offline, and you can also ensure that Explorer starts offline. Click the *Work Offline* item in the File menu of Explorer. This will allow you to work offline until you need to connect to the Web, and unless you remove the tick against this option, Explorer will always start in offline mode. You can use the *History* icon on the toolbar to recover previously downloaded material. Material received on the *Channels* will be stored until it is replaced by new materials, but you can specify the life of *History* pages, typically as 30 days.

Explorer bar: You can use the left-hand side of the screen, the Explorer bar, to hold a selected type of information. Click View — Explorer bar and select *Search*, *Favorites*, *History* or *Channels*. You can also click on *None* to remove this bar. Note that the same bar appears in Windows Explorer.

Buttons

General: Windows 98 makes more use of buttons than older Windows versions, because this fits in well with the principle of using a single click for a command.

Start: The *Start* button on the Taskbar is used to gain rapid access to programs and document files. If you have opted for a hidden Taskbar, you will have to move the cursor to the bottom of the screen to see the *Start* button (unless you have moved the taskbar to another side). See the entry for **Start** button for details.

Appearance: You can change the appearance of buttons by using the Display properties — Appearance. Look for the items *3D Objects* and *Caption Buttons*. You can alter the colour of 3D objects and the size and font for caption buttons.

Window buttons: Each window uses buttons at the top right hand corner for *Close*, *Minimize* and *Maximize* actions. You can carry out the same actions by clicking on the icon at the top left-hand corner of the window and selecting from the menu.

Any Window can be reduced to a button on the Taskbar by using the *Minimize* button of that window. You can minimise all windows by clicking with the right-hand mouse button on an unused part of the Taskbar and selecting *Minimize all Windows*. This can be undone by clicking again with the right hand mouse button on an unused portion of the Taskbar and selecting *Undo Minimize All*.

Mouse buttons: You can reverse your mouse button actions by opening the Control Panel and clicking on *Mouse*. The *Buttons* tab contains the options for *Left Hand* or *Right Hand* mouse operation.

Cache

General: The main cache for Windows 98 is set up when you install Windows, using the SMARTDRV.EXE program. You should not try to alter the action of this cache. The caches for Internet Explorer are files held in the folder C:\WINDOWS\Temporary Internet Files of your computer's hard drive. The size of these caches determines how many pages you can store, and so affects the number of times you can use the forward and back buttons. The caches are used particularly when you are downloading files, and for storing cookies (short information files that identify you to Web sites).

Changing Internet cache size: From Internet Explorer click View — Options. You will see the default *General* tab with the *Temporary Internet Files* section. Click the *Settings* button to see the percentage of hard drive space that can be assigned to these files. To alter the cache size, drag the slider in the direction of more or less hard drive space as required. A larger cache setting will speed up the viewing of pages that have already been downloaded, but if you are short of hard drive space you may want to decrease the cache size. You can clear **some** of these files (not cookies) by clicking the *Delete Files* button.

Folder actions: The default folder for the cache is C:\WINDOWS\Temporary Internet Files, and you may want to change this (for example, to a second larger hard drive). To do this, click the *Move Folder* button and browse to another drive or folder. The new folder will not be used until you re-boot the computer. You can view the files in the cache by clicking on *View files*. The *View Objects* button allows you to see what active content has been downloaded.

Note that you will be warned about deleting cookies if you start to delete files in the cache. You might want to arrange files in time order, before deleting any, so that you know which are the oldest files. If you have at some stage filled in details of your name, address and so on, then deleting the cookie in which these are held will mean that you will have to repeat the entry if you contact the same site again.

Updating cache: The cache is never totally cleared unless you use the *Delete files* button on the *General* tab — note that this does not delete cookies which are also held in the C:\Windows\Cookies folder. The pages may become out of date, particularly if they contain information that is likely to change rapidly, and you can use one of three options for updating pages. The default is to check the stored pages each time you start Internet Explorer, using the *Settings* button on the *General* tab. This will cause a short delay at startup, but will allow you to browse rapidly once any updating has been done.

There are two other options. One is never to update pages. This is useful if you are certain that the information is unchanging, and it provides the fastest access. The other option is to update on each visit to a page. This is useful if the information changes rapidly, but it makes browsing slower because each page has to be checked for new information.

Calculator

General: The Calculator utility of Windows 98 can be used as an on-screen simple arithmetical calculator, or as a full scientific calculator. The advantage, as compared to a hand-held calculator, is that the input and output numbers can be cut and pasted to and from other Windows 98 programs and documents. The Calculator program has been updated in Windows 98 to provide more precise results.

Launching: Start Calculator by clicking on its icon in the Start — Programs — Accessories menu. If Calculator is not in the *Start* menu, find the file by using Explorer, and click on the name. You can use the Settings — Taskbar option of the *Start* menu to place the Calculator icon and shortcut into the Accessories set. The Calculator window **cannot** be re-sized, but it can be minimised or moved. You can use the calculator either by clicking on the displayed keys, or using equivalent keyboard keys (see later for the list of keys for items other than numbers or simple arithmetic).

Display: The Calculator display can be toggled between *Standard* and *Scientific* (click in the *View* menu). The *Standard* calculator has the key arrangement of an ordinary pocket calculator with square root, percentage and inverse

(1/x) keys, along with the usual memory keys MC, MR, MS and M+, meaning memory clear, memory recall, memory store and memory add, respectively. The *Backspace* key, not generally available on a pocket calculator, will strip digits from a number starting from the right hand side, and is used to reduce the number of decimal places.

The *Scientific* calculator uses an extended keyboard (though, oddly, without the square root key) to provide a full set of scientific and statistical functions. The use of these functions is beyond the scope of this book and, in general, if you need the *Scientific* calculator you will have had experience of using these functions on a pocket scientific calculator. You can use the x^y key with y = ½ for a square root action.

- The Scientific calculator deals with functions (such as sin, exponent, etc.) following the usual scheme used on hand-held scientific calculators of requiring you to enter the number followed by the function. For example, for Sin(30) you enter 30 and then press the Sin button.

Cut and Paste: You can type a calculation in Notepad, copy and paste it to Calculator, and then copy and paste the result back to Notepad. You must enter the calculation in correct format into Notepad (for example. **4.75*3.14=** to multiply these numbers, or **5.7*4.5=@** to multiply and then take a square root on the *Standard* calculator), and a list follows of the key equivalents that can be used on the Calculator and in Notepad typing.

Key equivalents of buttons: The following list applies to the *Scientific* calculator, but apart from square root and percentage, the *Standard* calculator uses the same keys for the same buttons. The @ key is used for square root on the *Standard* calculator, which also uses the % key for percentages.

Windows 98 assistant

Button	Key	Button	Key	Button	Key	Button	Key
%	%	Back	BACK	Hyp	h	Pi	p
(	(	Bin	F8	Ln	n	Rad	F3
)	)	Byte	F4	Int	;	s	Ctrl-d
*	*	C	Esc	Inv	I	Sin	s
+	+	CE	Del	log	l	inv x^2	I@
+/–	F9	Cos	o	Lsh	<	Sta	Ctrl-s
–	–	Dat	Ins	M+	Ctrl-p	Sum	Ctrl-t
.	. or,	Dec	F6	MC	Ctrl-l	Tan	t
/	/	Deg	F2	Mod	%	Word	F3
dms	m	MR	Ctrl-r	Xor	^	1/x	r
Dword	F2	MS	Ctrl-m	x^2	@	=	Enter
Exp	x	n!	!	x^3	#	F-E	v
Not	~	x^y	y	And	&	Grad	F4
Oct	F7	Ave	Ctrl-a	Hex	F5	Or	l

Notes: Results on the *Standard* calculator are printed using up to 33 places of decimals , and you **cannot** use the *Backspace* button to reduce the number of decimal places. This can make the use of the calculator very clumsy as compared to a handheld type.

Capturing

General: Any complete screen or window can be captured to the Clipboard by using the *Print Screen* key. The Clipboard image can then be loaded into any bitmap editor, such as Paint, to be saved, edited and printed as required.

Action: Pressing the *Print Screen* key by itself will copy the entire screen display to the Clipboard. Using the *Alt* key along with the *Print Screen* key will capture the current Window, if more than one window is being displayed.

Using an image: A captured image can be pasted directly into a Word document, using the Edit — Paste command, or by the same method into Paint or any other bitmap graphics package. The Windows pointer does not appear in the captured image.

Notes: Working with screen images is faster and easier if the standard VGA 640 × 480, 16-colour screen is used. The captured images from screens that use higher resolution and/or larger numbers of colours are very much larger and need a fast processor to work with.

Some graphics packages, such as Paint Shop Pro 4.0, allow you to use a *Capture* utility that will capture the cursor, using a key of your choice (such as F12) to activate the action. These also offer the option of capturing the pointer image.

Printer port: If you work over a network, you can capture a printer port, meaning that the printer, wherever it may be, cannot be used by anyone else on the network. To capture the port, use Control Panel and Printers, and bring up the *Properties* for your printer, then click *Details* and *Capture Printer Port*. You can then select the port you want to capture and type the network path, and then select the port you captured in the *Print To The Following Port* box.

Text in dialogue box: To capture text in a Windows dialogue box, select the text and click with the right-hand mouse button, then click *Copy*. You can then paste the text into another application.

Cascading/tiling windows

General: When several windows are in use, they can be *cascaded* or *tiled*. Cascaded windows overlap, with one window shown entirely and the header bars of the others visibly stacked behind it. Tiled windows are arranged so that the whole of each window can be seen, with each window in a reduced size. Tiling can be horizontal (each window is a horizontal strip) or vertical (each window is a vertical strip).

Cascading: The windows must be open and not minimised. Click any blank portion of the Taskbar using the right-hand mouse button. From the menu that appears, click *Cascade* if you want to cascade the windows, otherwise select *Tile Horizontally* or *Tile Vertically*.

Restoring windows: You can close the cascaded or tiled windows that you do not need by clicking on the close icon (× symbol) at the top right hand corner of the header bar. If you want to restore the windows to their original state, click again on a blank portion of the Taskbar using the right-hand mouse button, and from the menu select *Undo Cascade/Tile*.

Notes: If you are using a Help screen, it will remain on top rather than being cascaded unless you have disabled the (default) *Help on Top* option.

Tiling is more useful on large monitor sizes, cascading on the smaller screen sizes.

CD-ROM drive

General: If a CD-ROM drive was installed in your computer before Windows 98 was installed, the CD-ROM drive will have been detected and correctly installed into the Windows system. If you install a modern CD-ROM drive *after* having installed Windows 98 you should allow

Windows to detect the drive rather than using the processes (such as altering the CONFIG.SYS file) that were used for installation using DOS or Windows 3.1. Windows 98 supports the use of CDs with more than 4 Gbyte capacity, and also DVD drives.

Installation: If you need to install a new CD-ROM drive to run under Windows 98, make certain that the hardware part of the installation (locating drive, connecting cables) is correctly carried out with the power off. Start the computer and then shut down any programs other than Explorer and Systray (see the entry for **Shut down**). Click the Start button and then Settings — Control Panel. Alternatively, if you are running Explorer, click the Control Panel item in the Explorer list. Click the *Add New Hardware* item, and start the Wizard running. Opt to allow Windows to find the new hardware (this is more likely to ensure correct installation) and when the searching process starts, wait until the action is completed. When the Wizard is finished, the CD-ROM drive should be correctly installed. This may call for a disc of software to be inserted.

Windows 98 contains a generic CD-ROM driver (ATAPI2CD.SYS) that is placed on the Startup disc so that the CD-ROM drive will be available even if the files on the hard drive cannot be used. For normal use, however, you should use the software installation that comes with the drive on a floppy. Once this has been run, you will be able to make use of the CD-ROM drive for other software installation.

Configuring: When a CD-ROM drive has been installed, you need to configure it for the performance you want. If you are using it in conjunction with a sound card and loudspeakers, you may want to use *AutoPlay*, so that inserting an audio CD will start that disc playing. See the **CD Player** entry for details. The other configuration action is to make the best possible use of the drive you have installed. Drives are classed by speed relative to ordinary audio CDs, and speeds such as 16×, 24×, and more are common. Lower speeds such as 6× are now confined to read/write CD drives.

The speed needs to be recognised by Windows. Click on Start — Settings — Control Panel or click on the Control Panel item of Explorer. Click on System — Performance — File System — CD ROM to see the CD ROM performance panel. Look for the *Access Pattern* box, and click the arrowhead to see the list of drive speeds. Click on the drive speed (usually *Quad-speed or higher*) that you are using. This will set the size of memory cache that the drive uses. To increase this further, drag the arrow indicator on the *Supplemental Cache Size* indicator closer towards the *Large* side (right hand side). If you have a memory size of 16 Mbyte or more you can drag the slider all the way to the *Large* side, providing 1238 Kbyte (1.2 Mbyte) of cache memory.

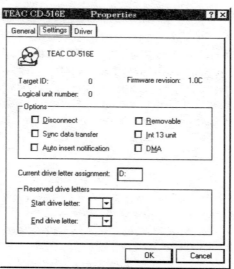

Device settings: You should also check device settings. Start the Control Panel — System from the *Start* button or the Explorer, and select the *Device Manager* tab. On this list of devices, click on *CD-ROM* and then click on the name of the drive that appears. Click the *Properties* button and on the two-tab panel that appears, click on *Settings*. The *Options* in this panel are normally made for you by Windows when the drive is installed, but you might want to make certain that the *Auto Insert Notification* is ticked. You can also check the drive letter and, if necessary, change it (unless this portion is greyed out). You can also specify a range of letters to be reserved for the CD-ROM drive.

If a box marked DMA appears, you should tick this. You will see a warning notice about incompatible devices, but if your CD-ROM drive cannot support DMA (a fast data transfer system) then the box will be automatically cleared later when you next start your computer. If the box remains ticked, data transfer from the CD-ROM drive will be much faster.

- Users of SCSI drives should check that the other options are also ticked, and the *Disconnect* option is set for IDE and EIDE drive connections.

Using CD-ROM: You will normally use CD-ROM for program installation or as a data source for an installed program. When you need to install a program, insert the CD disc and click the *Add/Remove Programs* item in the Control Panel. Follow the Wizard instructions, but if the CD-ROM is not recognised you can use the *Browse* action to locate the CD-ROM drive letter and find the INSTALL or SETUP program for the new software.

- When you need to use the CD for data, running its associated program (such as Encarta, for example) will automatically make use of the CD.

Notes: If you have installed programs that use the CD as a data source and you subsequently change the CD-ROM drive letter you may need to re-install the programs, as they will try to use the old drive letter. For example, if your CD-ROM drive used the letter D, and you subsequently install a new hard drive, this will force the CD-ROM drive to use the letter E (or higher, if the new hard drive is partitioned), and this new letter will not necessarily be recognised by some of your existing software.

- Even if a program makes considerable use of a CD-ROM for data, it will usually require space on the hard drive. For example, Encarta requires some 6 Mbyte of hard drive space.

CD Player

General: CD Player allows you to play your CD recordings on a computer that is equipped with a CD-ROM drive, a sound card, and loudspeakers (or earphones). You can opt for *AutoPlay*, so that a CD will start to play whenever you insert the disc in the drive.

Autoplay: To set AutoPlay, open Explorer and then click View — Folder options — File Types. Find the *Type* called *AudioCD* and click the *Edit* button. The word *Play* should appear in the *Actions* list. Click on this word and then click the *Set Default* button.

If the word *Play* is **not** on the *Actions* list, click the *Edit* button on the *Actions:* panel, and click in the *Action* panel that now appears. Type the word *Play*, and then move to the *Application used to perform this action* panel. Use the Browse key to find the program CDPLAYER.EXE (usually in the C:\WINDOWS folder), and click. When this panel is complete, click on *Play* and *Set Default* as noted above.

- You can remove the AutoPlay action from the same menu by clicking on *Play* and then on the *Remove* button.

- You can also temporarily disable the AutoPlay action if you hold down the Shift key when you load in an audio CD.

Using CD Player: The CD Player panel provides information on the audio CD that has been inserted, with a large (but not bright) display of time, and strips for *Artist*, *Title*, and *Track*. If no disc has been inserted the *Artist* text will read: *Data or no disc loaded*, meaning that you have either inserted no disc or that you have used a CD-ROM with no music content. If no disc has been inserted, the *Title* bar will read: *Please insert an audio compact disc*.

The icons next to the time display are the usual (video recorder style) play, pause, stop, previous track, skip backwards, skip forwards, next track, and eject actions.

The icons above the timer panel are for *Edit play list*, *Show elapsed track time*, *Show remaining track time*, *Show remaining disc time*, *Play tracks at random*, *Continuous play*, and *Play start of each track* respectively. These items are also available from the *Disk*, *View* and *Options* menus.

Editing Play list data: Currently, music CDs do not contain track data, but you can enter such data into a file on the hard drive that will be loaded when your CD is identified. This is done through the *Play list* when an audio disc has been loaded. When you click on the icon or the menu item, you will see a panel that contains lines marked *Drive*, *Artist* and *Title*, and you can enter your own text into the *Artist* and *Title* lines. Below these is space for the *Play List* and *Available Tracks*, used for display only. You can enter information for each track on the bottom line which will initially be marked as *Track 01*. When you have typed data, click the *Set Name* key to add the information to the *Play List* and *Available Tracks* list.

Making a Play List: The default *Play List* consists of all tracks in sequence. You can select a track by clicking in the *Play List* and remove it by clicking on the *Remove* button, and you can add a track by clicking on a name in the *Available Tracks* list and clicking on the *Add* button. In this way, you can make up a play list of your own, and you can add a track more than once. If necessary, you can delete the entire *Play* list by clicking on the *Clear All* button. You can replace all tracks in the *Play List* (using the *Available Tracks* list) by clicking the *Reset* button. You can also alter the order of tracks in the *Play List* by dragging track titles from one position to another.

Options: The Options — Preferences menu item allows you to select each of the following: *Stop CD Player on Exit, Save Settings on Exit* and *Show Tool Tips*. You can also change the default time of 15 seconds gap between tracks.

Notes: See also the entries for **Volume control, Media devices**.

Channels

General: You normally have to seek out Internet information for yourself by browsing. The *Channels* system allows you to select from a long list of sources (Channels) which consist of providers that will download updated information to you when you start Explorer online. When you subscribe to a Channel (this does not involve payment) you ensure that the contents are automatically updated each time you make contact. You can see a Channel content without subscribing, but you will not be able to set your own schedule for updating unless you subscribe. You can add

Channels to your set (on the Channel bar) without subscribing, so that you can look up information in some channels at intervals without needing to waste time downloading it each time you use Channels. Channels are obtained through the Microsoft Web site.

Subscribing: Click the Channels button (icon of satellite dish) on your Taskbar and then click Channel Guide. Follow the instructions that appear on the screen.

Displaying: Click the Channels button on the Taskbar, and select the Channel name that you want, such as *Teletext Direct*. The channels are normally displayed in a vertical list (the Channel bar) on the left-hand side of the screen, with the information over the remainder of the screen. When this bar is used for other purposes it is called the Explorer bar.

Options: You can display Channel information (either static or altering) on the Desktop or as a Screen-saver. The information will change only while you are online.

Note: You can obtain the Channel bar on Windows Explorer or on Internet Explorer.

Character map

General: The Character map is used to insert symbols and foreign characters into text and is available for use by programs that run under Windows 98. For example, Word-97 can use the Character map by way of its Insert — Symbol menu. For other programs such as Wordpad, you can call up the Character Map display and use it as described here.

Launching: If Character Map was installed with Windows, 98 you can launch it by using Start — Programs — Accessories and clicking on *Character Map*. If this does not exist, check that the file CHARMAP.EXE appears in the

Windows 98 assistant

C:\WINDOWS folder. You can click this name to launch Character Map, or make a shortcut to it.

If Character Map is not present in your system, you can use Windows 98 Setup and specify that you want to install this program only, see the entry for **Installing Windows 98 components.**

Using: Select from the *Font* list the font set from which you want to take special characters. This will usually be the font you are currently using if you want to add accented characters, or the *Symbol* or *Wingdings* fonts for Greek, mathematical and other symbols. Use *System* or *Terminal* fonts if you want to match the use of these fonts in graphics programs. If you have a large number of installed fonts, you will find them all available in the Character Map list. Some of these fonts will have been added by other applications.

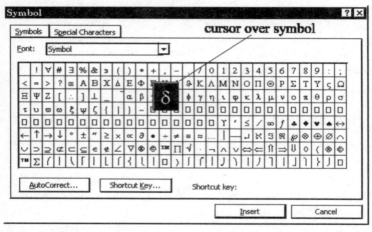

With the correct font in use, click on the character you want to add, or single-click on the character and then click on the *Select* button.. You can see that character magnified if you hold down the mouse button before double-clicking. Each double-clicked character will appear in the *Characters to copy* space and you can place a number of consecutive characters into this space. Click the *Copy* button when you are ready, and then switch back to the document that you are working on. Place the cursor and click in the position where you want the character to appear, then click Edit — Paste. If the characters change when you *Paste* them in, select them, and then change to the font that you used in the Character Map. If your subsequent typing makes use of characters that are not on your keyboard, select them and change back to your original font.

Notes: Character Map **cannot** be used on programs that run under DOS. If you are using Word, the method of inserting characters makes use of the Character Map display, but is simpler – the character is inserted automatically with no need to use the *Copy* and *Paste* actions.

If you insert characters using Charmap and then save a file in ASCII (txt) format, the inserted characters will not appear correctly in the file when you open it to read again. This applies also to files that are sent as email using TXT rather than HTML format.

Clipboard Viewer

General: The Clipboard Viewer allows you to see what is contained in the Clipboard memory before you paste it into another document. It also provides for saving the clipboard contents (and re-loading them) if you wish, though this facility is seldom used. Clipboard Viewer is available only if it was installed as one of the Accessories when Windows 98 was set up on your computer. See the entry for **Installing Windows 98 components** for adding this and other accessories. The file is **clpbrd.exe**, in the C:\Windows folder.

Use: When you use Start — Programs — Accessories — Clipboard Viewer you will see the Clipboard Viewer panel appear as a small window which can be moved and/or re-sized as required. If anything has been captured to the Clipboard, it will appear in the *Viewer* panel.

Save and Open: Any information in the Clipboard can be saved by using the File — Save As option. This will save the information as a CLP file which can later be opened from Clipboard. This facility is seldom needed, because most captured images are pasted into other documents and saved as part of such documents.

File Conversion: Information in the Clipboard can be converted to another format, and the permitted formats depend on whether text or graphics is being used. Click the *Display* menu heading to see the permitted formats.

Notes: Clipboard Viewer is of little use if you use the Clipboard predominantly as an intermediate in cut and paste actions and unless you find the *Save As* or the *Conversion* options useful you need not install the Clipboard Viewer.

Clock

General: The Clock utility of Windows 98 provides a digital time display on the Taskbar, unlike the window display of the clock in Windows 3.1. The Taskbar clock icon can also provide date information.

Setting up: Click Start — Settings — Taskbar and in the *Taskbar Options* panel, click the selection box marked *Show Clock*. This will ensure that the time display appears in the Taskbar.

Use: You can read the time from the Taskbar display, and if you hold the pointer on this display, the date will appear also.

Options: Click the time display on the Taskbar, using the right-hand mouse button. You can then select *Adjust Date/Time* from the menu. Alternatively, double-click the time display using the left-hand mouse button. You can also adjust the *Time Zone* from this display.

Notes: The Date/Time and Time Zone can also be changed from the Control Panel — Date/Time option.

Colours

General: The number of colours that you can use depends on what range your monitor and your graphics card will permit, and on the speed you want to achieve on your computer. Using the standard 16-colour and 640 × 480 resolution display on the monitor ensures that programs which make use of screen images will run as fast as possible. For better appearance of pictures you may want to use the higher options for colours, such as *256*, *High Colour* (16-bit, equal to 65536 colours) or *True Colour* (24-bit or 32-bit, for photographic quality), but using these options will noticeably slow down your work unless you are using a very fast machine with a graphics accelerator card that contains a generous amount of memory, typically 2 Mbyte or more. In addition, images in *True Colour* will demand a very large amount of hard drive and memory space.

Colour settings: Save data and close down all programs except Explorer. Click Start — Settings — Control Panel, or click Control Panel from the Explorer display. Click on the *Display* icon and then select the *Settings* tab. On this panel, select the *Colour Palette* setting that you want from the set that appears when you click the arrowhead. When you click the *OK* button you will be notified that you must restart the computer for the new settings to take effect. Remember that the higher settings such as *High Colour* and *True Colour* can be used only if your monitor supports them.

- Some monitors do not need a restart for colour changes. On the Display Properties — General tab, click the *Advanced* button. This brings up another set of tabs, and in the *General* set you will see the option to show settings in the task bar, and a set called *Compatibility*. In this set, you can click the option marked *Apply the new color settings without restarting*. This will have no effect unless your monitor/graphics card is a modern type.

- The resolution settings for the monitor can also be changed in this panel by dragging the *Desktop Area* slider to one of the other settings. The standard settings are 640 × 480, 800 × 600 and 1024 × 768. As for colours, the higher settings are available only if your monitor supports them.

- Some graphics card/monitor combinations can place a *Display* icon in the Taskbar, see above. This icon can be clicked once to show a list of available settings, and double-clicked to bring up the *Display* panel without using Control Panel.

Colour scheme: You can select the colours that are used for different parts of the Windows display. Use the Control Panel — Display option as above and click the *Appearance* tab. This opens a panel that displays the appearance of a typical window. You can click on any part of this display to see the name appear in the *Item* panel, along with entries in the *Size* and *Colour* boxes. This allows you to change the size, colour and font used for any part of a typical window display.

You can select from a range of preset displays. These are named, but the names are not necessarily a useful guide to their appearance. The current set of names is as follows, omitting the large number of *High Contrast* schemes that are intended for visually impaired users. The abbreviations L, EL and HC mean Large, Extra Large and High Colour respectively. The HC options require a *High Color (16-bit)* setting in the *Colors* section.

Brick	Desert	Eggplant
Lilac	Lilac (L)	Maple
Marine (HC)	Plum (HC)	Pumpkin (L)
Rainy Day	Red, White & Blue (VGA)	Rose
Rose (L)	Slate	Spruce
Storm (VGA)	Teal (VGA)	Wheat
Windows Standard	Windows Standard (EL)	Windows Standard (L)

- The larger sizes are useful when you are using the higher screen resolution figures.

You can create your own set of colours by selecting a colour for each portion of the display from the *Item* set, and assigning a colour from the list. The number of colours that you can select from depends on which colour options (16, 256, etc.) that you have set in the *Colour Palette*, and includes some grey or shaded options. Having created a display in this way, you can save it using a filename of your own by clicking the *Save As* button.

- If you use a filename with no capital letters you can easily distinguish your own colour sets from these supplied with Windows.

The standard portions of a window are:

Windows 98 assistant

3-D Objects	Active Title Bar	Active Window Border
Application Background	Caption Buttons	Desktop
Icon	Icon Spacing (Horizontal)	Icon Spacing (Vertical)
Inactive Title Bar	Inactive Window Border	Menu
Message Box	Palette Title	Scrollbar
Selected Items	Tooltip	Window

- Remember that you can also change the fonts that are used for each portion of a Window display. The standard font is the MS Sans Serif, but you may prefer the appearance of some of the other fonts that you have on your hard drive. You can also change font size in Help windows using the *Options* button and selecting *Font*.

Note: If you are using screen-grabs to illustrate a document, it's often better to use colour schemes that use a set of grey shades or colours to provide good contrast, particularly if the document will be printed on a monochrome printer.

- These colour schemes are used only for Windows programs, and will not appear in MS-DOS programs that you run using Windows 98.

Colours, Web pages

General: You can opt to use the colours that are set by your Windows settings, or for foreground and background colours that are specific to your Internet Explorer display. This will not necessarily change some of the colours (or fonts) that are used in pages you download. See also the **fonts** entry.

Changing colours: Click Internet Explorer View — Options — General. Click the button labelled *Colors*. If *Use Windows colors* is ticked, you can click to remove this so that you can specify your own colours for the *Text* and *Background* options. For each option, click on the rectangle to obtain a colour palette, and then click on the colour that you want to use. You can also specify *Define Custom Colors*, creating your own colours by pointing to a colour triangle or by entering colour specifications in terms of red, blue and green; or the alternative specification of hue, saturation and luminance. In general, these latter settings are useful only if you are interested in matching colours for which you have a specification using the same system.

Config.sys file

General: The CONFIG.SYS file is used during the process of starting up the computer, and is a file of commands that are executed before Windows 98 can be initiated. Another such file is called **AUTOEXEC.BAT**. You should not, in normal circumstance, need to edit or view the CONFIG.SYS file, because it is maintained automatically by Windows 98. If your computer was in use before Windows 98 was installed (using Windows 3.1 or DOS) then several portions of the file will have been modified by the installation program for Windows 98.

Editing: Start Notepad and use the Open command to look for all files (*.*). Look in the C:\ root folder and click CONFIG.SYS. The file can then be edited. See *BP319 MS-DOS 6 explained* for details of how to use this file.

Bypassing: If a command in the CONFIG.SYS file is causing problems with Windows 98, you can start the computer in such a way as to bypass the commands. Depending on your computer type, you can use either the left Ctrl key or the F8 key while starting. Restart the computer, and hold down whichever of these keys is effective in preventing Windows from loading. From the menu that appears, select *Step by Step Confirmation*. This allows you to accept or reject each step in the setup, starting with the CONFIG.SYS file. The final step should be the AUTOEXEC.BAT file (or Startup Command File, as it is referred to). If you do not use this file, you can avoid starting Windows 98 and the machine will be running DOS.

Notes: If you have never used DOS, and particularly if your computer was installed with Windows 98 when you bought it, you should never need to edit AUTOEXEC.BAT or CONFIG.SYS, and you should certainly not do so unless you understand the effects that changes in these files could cause.

Content type

General: When a file is down loaded, Internet Explorer can recognise the type of file and call up a program to read it, providing that this content type has been notified. Files that are or can be, recognised by Internet Explorer are recognised by their MIME — Multipurpose Internet Mail Extension — letters, such as JPE for a JPEG compressed image file. You can define a new extension so that the correct program will be called up, or you can change the program that will deal with an existing file type. The default types cover audio (sound), image, text and video files. Note that you really need to know something about file types and such topics as DDE before you attempt to create new types of edit existing ones. Virtually all the files currently in use are already set up for you.

New file type: If a file is downloaded and cannot be read, its file type will have to be notified. Click Windows Explorer View — Folder Options and click the *File types* tab. Click on the *New Type* button, and fill in the details on the page that appears. You can change the icon for the file by clicking on the *Change icon* button.

The *Description of Type* line can be filled in with a note of your own, or left blank. The *Associated extension* will be whatever appears as the file extension. The *Content type* (MIME) line must contain the correct description for this file type, and a list of recognised types, see below, will appear when you click the arrowhead. If the new file is not on this list you will have to devise another content line for it. Finally, you have to add the *Actions* that you want to be performed on the file. If nothing appears here, use the *New* button to add an action such as **Open** or **Print**. If an existing action seems inappropriate, you can click the *Edit* button to alter it.

Recognised types: The list of recognised content types is:

application/msword	application/x-cdf
application/x-compress	application/x-compressed
application/x-gzip	application/x-internet-signup
application/x-tar	application /x-x509-ca-cert
application/x-zip-compressed	audio /aiff
audio /basic	audio /wav
audio /x-aiff	audio /x-pn-realaudio
image/bmp	image/gif

image /jpeg	image /pcx
image/pipeg	image/tiff
image/x-jg	image/x-xbitmap
message/rfc822	text /html
text /plain	video/mpeg
video /vdo	video/x-ivf
video/x-msvideo	x-world/x-vrml

Alter content type: Click the Edit button on the File Types panel, and alter whichever of the items that you want to change. The list starts with *Application used to perform action*, and this is often **Windows Explorer** when an **Open** command is used. The rest of the panel is relevant only if the DDE option is ticked, and these lines must not be changed unless you understand what the DDE action is and how it can be modified. The editable lines are headed *DDE Message, Application, DDE Application not running*, and *Topic*. Unless you have programming skills or have been advised how to change DDE items, leave this set alone.

Context-sensitive Help

General: Much of the Help action in Windows 98 is context-sensitive, meaning that the help you get is related to the action you are trying to carry out at the time. The **?** icon at the top right-hand corner of a panel is used for this type of Help.

Seeking Help: Click on the **?** icon. The **?** sign will now appear next to the normal pointer, and you can click on the portion of the panel that you do not understand. A small explanatory panel will appear as a reminder of what to expect. An alternative is a Help menu item called *What's This*.

Notes: This type of Help is a very useful reminder, but it is necessarily brief, and is not useful if you are totally unfamiliar with the program actions that you are using.

Copying

General: The normal *Cut/Copy* and *Paste* actions are provided in the *Edit* menu of any program running under Windows, but Windows also permits the use of the right-hand mouse button for a shortcut menu, and also the use of Drag and Drop editing in many programs. For a definition, see the entry for **object**. Note that the action described as *Move* is a copy action followed by deletion of the original object.

Shortcut menus: With some object (text, graphics, etc.) selected, click the right-hand mouse button over the selected area. You will see a short menu of the most-often-required actions. For text, this menu will typically be *Cut*, *Copy*, *Paste*, *Font*, *Paragraph*, *Bullets and Numbering*, and for graphics it will typically be *Cut*, *Copy*, *Paste*, *Format Drawing Object*, *Bring to Front*, *Send to Back*, *Send Behind Text*, *Group* and *Ungroup*. You can click *Copy* or *Cut* to copy selected text (using *Cut* will remove the text from its present position, making the *Cut* and *Paste* action a *Move*), and by clicking with the right-hand mouse button over another point in the document you can click the *Paste* portion of the menu and so paste in the copied material. The *Paste* action can be repeated.

Drag and Drop: This action may need to be enabled for a specific program (for Word, in the Tools — Options — Edit menu) and is not available in some other older programs (such as Windows Notepad). If *Drag and Drop* is available, select the text or graphics and keep the left-hand mouse button depressed until the cursor changes shape to its *Drag and Drop* form. Now drag the selected text or graphics to its new position, then release the mouse button. The action is normally a *Move* (*Cut* and *Paste*) type, but if you press the Ctrl key and hold it down during the dragging action, the action will be a *Copy* and *Paste*, so that the original text or graphic is not deleted. The use of *Drag and Drop* is less attractive when the text or graphics object has to be moved over a large number of pages.

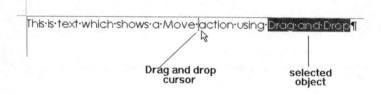

This·is·text·which·shows·a·Move·action·using·Drag·and·Drop¶

Drag and drop
cursor

selected
object

Discs: You can opt to copy a file or folder to a floppy disc. Select the file or folder by placing the pointer over it and then click File — Sent To and click the floppy drive in this menu.

Help topics: You can copy any Help topic by clicking the right-hand mouse button with the pointer inside the Help window, and then clicking *Copy*. You can also click the *Copy* item in the *Edit* or *Options* set. Select text if you do not want to copy the complete item. Paste the item where you want it to appear.

Scraps: Select the item (text or graphics) you want to copy and drag it to the Desktop. This scrap can be dragged to another program or document later — it can be left on the desktop if needed and copied indefinitely. This is not so useful if you use the Web-style desktop with no icons visible.

MSDOS text: You can copy text from an MS-DOS program in an MS-DOS window. Click the MS-DOS icon, point to *Edit* and click *Mark*. Click on the start of the text, hold down the Shift key and then click at the end of the text. Now click *Edit* and *Copy*. Paste the item where you want it to appear.

Window content: Press the Print Screen key to copy the whole screen to the Clipboard, or use Alt–Print Screen to copy the active window. Paste into a graphics program of the bitmap type.

Copying, Internet pages

General: Internet pages are in HTML format, and to copy information from a Web page into another document (not another Web page, however) you should use the Copy and Paste actions.

Copying: Select the data, or use Edit — Select All for the whole document. Click Edit — Copy. Switch to (or open) the document that is to hold the data, and click on the place where you want to data to appear. Click Edit — Paste for the application that runs the document (such as Notepad or Word). You will not necessarily see all of the items on a page copied, only the plain text.

Note: The *Cut, Copy* and *Paste* actions in the Edit menu of Internet Explorer are intended for use with source code (click View — Source) for a page rather than for copying text. A copied page will show its hyperlinks, but these will not necessarily lead to a Web site when they are clicked in the copy.

If you opt to save a Web page to a file, you will have the choice of saving as HTML (with hyperlinks) or as plain text. If you use HTML, the links can still be used when you display the file on screen, but a file saved as text contains no links or text effects.

Country (regional) settings

General: Windows 98 can be adapted to cater for differences between countries, something that is not always noted in books that originate in the USA. You can configure Windows by way of the *Regional Settings* of date, time, number format and currency sign and conventions.

Language settings: Use Start — Settings — Control Panel, or click Control Panel from Explorer, and click on *Regional Settings*. The first tab deals with languages, offering the following main and auxiliary options:

Afrikaans	Albanian	Basque
Belarusian	Bulgarian	Catalan
Croatian	Czech	Danish
Dutch (Belgian)	Dutch (standard)	English (Australian)
English (Canadian)	English (Caribbean)	English (Ireland)
English (Jamaica)	English (New Zealand)	English (South Africa)
English (UK)	English (USA)	Estonian
Finnish	French (Belgian)	French (Canadian)
French (Luxembourg)	French (Standard)	French (Swiss)
German (Austria)	German (Liechtenstein)	German (Luxembourg)

Country (regional) settings

German (Standard)	German (Swiss)	Greek
Hungarian	Icelandic	Indonesian
Italian (Standard)	Italian (Swiss)	Latvian
Lithuanian	Macedonian (FYROM)	Norwegian (Bokmal)
Norwegian (Nynersk)	Polish	Portuguese (Brazilian)
Portuguese (Standard)	Romanian	Russian
Serbian (Cyrillic)	Slovak	Slovenian
Spanish (Argentina)	Spanish (Bolivia)	Spanish (Chile)
Spanish (Columbian)	Spanish (Costa Rica)	Spanish (Dominican Republic)
Spanish (Ecuador)	Spanish (El Salvador)	Spanish (Guatemala)
Spanish (Honduras)	Spanish (International)	Spanish (Mexico)
Spanish (Nicaragua)	Spanish (Panama)	Spanish (Paraguay)
Spanish (Peru)	Spanish (Puerto Rico)	Spanish (Traditional)
Spanish (Uruguay)	Spanish (Venezuela)	Swedish
Turkish	Ukranian	

Windows 98 assistant

Number settings: Several of the number settings, such as the use of a decimal point (rather than a comma) are fixed by your choice of language, but a few can be changed independently. The panel displays examples of both positive and negative numbers as examples. The sections of this panel are *Decimal Marker*, *Number of Digits following Decimal Marker*, *Digit Grouping Symbol*, *Number of Digits in Group*, *Negative Sign*, *Negative Number Format*, *Display Leading Zero*, *Measurement System* and *List Separator*.

Using the *English (UK) Language* setting, the default number of digits following the decimal point is 2, but you can select any number from 0 to 9. As noted earlier, these options do not apply to the Scientific Calculator. The digit grouping symbol is the comma, and the normal number of digits in a group is 3. The default negative number format uses the - sign ahead of the number, but you can opt for using brackets (for accountancy), to have the negative sign following the number, or to place a space between the negative sign and the number. There is no provision for using the longer – sign (the en-dash) that is usually required for mathematical typing in the UK, though this sign is available in Word and other programs that run using Windows 98.

Currency settings: Several of the currency settings are determined by the number settings which are in turn determined by language choice, and the only main item that can be varied is the negative number format, for which there are 15 options. The panel shows examples of positive and negative currency amounts and the options are *Currency Symbol*, *Position of Currency Symbol*, *Negative Number Format*, *Decimal Symbol*, *Number of Digits following Decimal Symbol*, *Digit Grouping Symbol* and *Number of Digits in Group*. The currency symbol can be deleted and another typed in — currently there is no provision for entering the Euro symbol directly, though you can enter the symbol in a document you edit in Word (using a Eurofont).

Time settings: The Panel shows an appearance sample, and for *English* (*UK*) language setting the options for *Time Display* are HH:mm:ss (24-hour clock) or H:mm:ss (12-hour clock with AM and PM). The *Time Separator* is set as a colon (:), and the AM and PM letterings are fixed by the language choice.

Date settings: The Date panel has a *Calendar Type* setting which is fixed at *Gregorian Calendar* for most language choices. The date options are grouped as *Short Date* or *Long Date*. The default *Short Date* style is dd/mm/yy, with three other options available, and the default separator is the slash (/). The *Long Date* has only the two options of dd MMMM yyyy or d MMMM yyyy.

Notes: Other than checking the current date and time and the language setting when you install Windows, you need not use the *Regional Settings* again unless you have special requirements, such as using brackets to indicate negative numbers in accountancy, or typing documents that are intended for other countries and which must use different number and/or currency formats. If you use an accounts program it will configure its numbers independently of Windows 98.

Date/Time

General: The maintenance and display of date and time is handled by the *real-time clock* of the computer, called thus to distinguish it from the clock circuits that are used to synchronise the microprocessor actions. When re-setting is needed, the Date/Time panel can be used. Windows 98 will automatically alter the time by one hour to adjust between Winter Time and Summer Time.

Windows 98 assistant

Display: Click Start — Settings — Taskbar Options. If the option marked *Show Clock* is ticked, the time will be displayed at the right hand side of the Taskbar. Placing the pointer over the time display will show the date in long form (such as 19 May 1998).

Adjusting: The simplest method is to double-click the time in the Taskbar display if you have used the *Show Clock* option, or click the time with the right-hand mouse button and opt for *Date/Time* in the menu that appears. Alternatively, use Explorer or My Computer to start the Control Panel and click *Date/Time*. You can change the year (beyond 2000 if required), month and day by clicking the arrowheads and the calendar display. To change time, click on the figure (hours, minutes or seconds) that you want to change and either click the arrowheads to adjust up or down or delete and type another number.

Time Zone: If you move to another time zone, click on this tab and select from the set of *Time Zones* that appears. The *Time Zones* are illustrated on a World map display, and also with examples of cities or countries in that time zone. The number of hours ahead of or behind GMT is also shown.

Summer Time: If you want Windows to change the hour automatically when Summer Time starts and ends, click the *Time Zone* tab and click to place a tick on the square labelled *Automatically adjust clock for daylight saving changes*.

Note: You can cause a number of bizarre effects if you change to a date far in the future. For example, changing the date to 2098 will cause long delays and error messages when starting Control Panel, and several other odd errors will also be encountered. Dates within the lifetime of Windows 98 cause no problems. You can usually assume that dates up to 2030 will cause no problems with modern software, but some programs will refuse to run if the clock is set beyond that date. Accounts programs that calculate the value of an investment at a future date should be checked carefully.

Defragmenter

Defragmenter notes: When a file is deleted, its codes remain on the disc, but the space can from then on be used to store other files, replacing the bytes of the deleted file. If, however, the replacement files do not take up the same amount of space, there will be portions of the disc that are unused, and if a large number of files are saved, deleted and then replaced, the disc will start to suffer from fragmentation.

On such a disc, saving a new file might make use of several portions of the disc that contained fragments of deleted files, and because the disc head has to move from portion to portion to read or write such a fragmented file, the time needed is longer. Defragmentation is a process which locates the fragments of files and stores them in adjacent parts of the disc, making access to such *contiguous files* quicker. To do this, files are read into memory and back to another part of the disc, and the whole process can take several hours on a large disc. Windows 98 caters for defragmentation by using the System Tools Defragmenter, which will also rearrange your files so that files you use frequently are loaded faster.

Starting: Close down all programs. This is important to avoid possible corruption. If you use a Screen Saver or monitor power shutdown system, switch it off (by specifying None). Click Start — Programs — Accessories — System Tools and then click on **Disk Defragmenter**. You will be asked which drive you want to defragment, the default is C:\. When you select a drive and click on the *OK* button, there will be a pause while the disc is checked, and a message will tell you how fragmented the disc is, and whether defragmentation is needed. If the fragmentation is 0% then you quite certainly do not need to use the defragmenter, but you may find that a drive with a fragmentation figure as low as 3% (with defragmentation not recommended in the message) can still show a gain in speed of use after defragmentation. Click the *Start* button to start the defragmentation of the selected disc.

Options: You can click the arrowhead next to the Drive display if you decide to defragment another drive instead (remember that if your hard drive is partitioned it will use more than one letter reference). Click the *Settings* button to see options for the defragmentation process itself. The choices of *Rearrange program files so my programs start faster* and *Check the drive for errors* are ticked by default, and you should leave these ticks in place unless you have some pressing reason to change them.

The lower part of the panel determines whether you use the options once only or each time the disc is defragmented. The default is to apply the settings each time.

Note: You can follow the progress of defragmentation if you want to by clicking the button in the Defragmenter panel. Click also the button marked *Legends* for an explanation of the symbols that are used to represent clusters of data on the disc.

- You **can** use the computer while defragmentation is proceeding, but there will be irritating pauses, and it is much better to start the process at a time when you do not need to use the computer. If you must use the computer, it is better to click the *Pause* button on the Defragmenter panel so that you can use the machine normally, with no hold-ups, and then resume the defragmentation action when you are not using the machine.

Note: If a screen saver starts during defragmentation and you click or use a key so as to see the screen again, you are likely to find that defragmentation starts all over again.

Deleting actions

General: You can delete text, files, folders, shortcuts and graphics. Unless you specify otherwise, deletion of objects is not permanent because they can be recovered from the Recycle Bin until the Bin is emptied. In other words, you do not clear any disc space by a delete action until the Recycle Bin is emptied. This provides for second thoughts if you need to replace something that you have deleted. Programs often have their own provision, such as the *Undo* icon of Word, for recovering deleted text or other items. You cannot delete the Recycle Bin but you can stop using it, see the entry for **Recycle Bin**.

Actions: All deletion starts with selection. Click on a file or folder name or on a graphic (so that the *handles* appear). If you work with the Desktop visible and the Recycle Bin displayed, you can drag the selected item to the Recycle Bin. If you work full-screen, which is more usual, press the Delete key. You will be asked to confirm that you want to send the selected item to the Recycle Bin.

• When you delete a folder you will automatically delete all the items that were contained in that folder. You will **not** be notified about individual items except for EXE files, to remind you that you are deleting a program which you might possibly want to use.

Permanent deletion: If you are certain that you want to delete an item and you need the disc space, hold down the Shift key while you drag the item to the *Recycle Bin* or press the Delete key. You will be reminded that this is a deletion as distinct from a recycling. In some cases, you may see the *Recycle Bin* notice appear, and you need to click the *No* button and use Shift–Delete again. See the entry for **Recycle Bin** for permanent deletion of the files in this set.

Desktop

General: The Desktop display of Windows 98 appears in full when you minimise all programs, and can be partially seen when you run programs in small windows. If you use full-screen for your main programs, the desktop will not normally be visible, so that its appearance is not relevant. In addition, if the Desktop is not visible, you cannot use options such as dragging a file to the Recycle Bin or to a Printer icon, etc. The Desktop appearance can be altered by using the *Wallpaper* option in the *Background* tab of Display Properties. The range of choices open to you may be determined by the options you used when setting up Windows 98.

You can also opt for an *Active Desktop*, meaning that the Desktop can be used to show material from the Web (which will change as long as you are connected online). You can also opt to use an Active Desktop without displaying Web material and to suppress the appearance of icons on the Active Desktop.

Background: Click Start — Settings — Control Panel, or use Control Panel from Explorer. Click the *Display* option, and click on the *Background* tab. The illustration shows the effect on a blank desktop of the type of background you select. The list, obtained by using the scroll bar in the *Wallpaper* box, consists of:

None	1stboot	Black Thatch
Blue Rivets	Bubbles	Carved Stone

Circles	Clouds	Forest
Gold Weave	Houndstooth	Metal Links
Pinstripe	Red Blocks	Sandstone
Setup	Stitches	Straw Mat
Tiles	Triangles	Waves
Windows 98		

The manufacturer of your computer may have added some additional background items.

The default for this *Wallpaper* is to tile it, meaning that the pattern repeats to cover the screen. The options are *Center* and *Stretch*. If you are using a larger picture with the *Center* option for your Wallpaper, you can opt to make a border by clicking the *Pattern* button. The standard set of patterns uses the names:

None	Bricks	Buttons
Cargo Net	Circuits	Cobblestones
Colosseum	Daisies	Dizzy
Field Effect	Key	Live Wire
Plaid	Rounder	Scales
Stone	Thatches	Tile
Triangles	Waffle's Revenge	

You can edit any selected design by using the *Edit Pattern* button. This will bring up a design of 8×8 squares. Click on a square to reverse its colour. When you have changed a pattern, you can click on the *Change* button to save this pattern under the existing filename. As an alternative, you can click the name and alter it, then use the *Add* button to add the new name for this altered pattern. If you want to delete a pattern, select it and click the *Remove* button. Click on the *Done* button to leave the editor panel.

Viewing Desktop: If your have covered the Desktop, you can view it by right-clicking in a vacant part of the Taskbar, and clicking on *Minimize All Windows*. You can return by repeating the right-click and selecting the *Undo Minimize All* option. Another route to the Desktop is to click the Desktop icon in the set at the left-hand side of the Taskbar (between Outlook Express and Channels).

Shortcuts on the Desktop: You can create shortcuts, placed on the Desktop, to any program or action or to a folder, floppy disc or printer. The easiest method is to minimise all programs other than Explorer, and use Explorer in a reduced window. Click the file, folder, program, printer or even another computer on a network, using the **right**-hand mouse button. When the menu appears, click *Make Shortcut*. For a file or folder, this will create a shortcut in the same folder that will appear selected, and you can then drag it to the Desktop. If you have selected a printer or disc then a notice will appear. The notice informs you that you cannot create the shortcut in the existing folder, and asks if you want it placed on the Desktop. Click the *Yes* button instead of dragging the shortcut to the Desktop.

For further information on Shortcuts, see the entry for **Shortcuts**. You can remove Shortcuts from the Desktop by selecting the shortcut and pressing the *Delete* key. This will send the Shortcut to the Recycle Bin. Alternatively, you can hold down the *Shift* key when you press *Delete* to make the deletion permanent.

Active desktop: If you did not initially opt for this, you can turn this on by clicking the desktop space using the right-hand mouse button, and selecting *Active Desktop* and then *View as Web Page*. Another route is by way of Start —

Settings — Active Desktop. This does **not**, by itself, add any Web material.

You can place Web material (such as Channel information) on the Desktop by clicking on the Desktop with the right-hand mouse button and selecting *Properties*. In this set, click *Web* and then *New*. You can then go online and browse the Active Desktop Gallery, or go to a Web site you prefer.

Another method that you can use while browsing the Web is to click any link on a Web page using the right-hand mouse button. You can then drag the link to the desktop, and then click *Create Active Desktop item(s) Here* to make this link your active desktop.

An active desktop display will remain unchanging while you are offline, and will be updated when you go online again. The Microsoft Active Desktop Gallery is of limited interest to UK viewers at the time of writing unless you want US items of news, weather or sport.

Dialler

General: Dialler is a utility that replaces older versions (such as the dialling utility of Windows 3.1 Cardfile) and allows you to dial numbers from your computer (if you have a modem). Numbers, up to eight, can be stored for rapid access, and you can also use a log facility to dial any number, either outgoing or incoming, that you have contacted earlier. If you did not opt for *Phone Dialer* when you installed Windows, you can add it using Control Panel — Add/Remove Programs — Windows Setup. You can then place *Phone Dialer* on your Start menu. The file is called **dialer.exe** and is in the C:\Windows folder.

Making a call: To make a call, start the dialler from Programs — Accessories — Communications and type the number into the space provided. If you have stored the number, click on the name that appears in the *Speed Dial* set. Click the *Dial* button to dial the number, and pick up the telephone handset when you are prompted.

Storing numbers: You can store the number that is the current *Number to Dial* by selecting the number, clicking Edit — Copy, then selecting a *Speed Dial* number and in the number space on the form use Shift — Insert to add the number. You can then type the name. To enter a set of names and numbers, click Edit — Speed Dial and fill in the information. Once names and numbers have been stored you can recall the number by using the appropriate *Speed Dial* number. Dialling is not carried out until the *Dial* button is clicked.

Using the log: With Dialler active, click on Tools — Show Log. This will display the Log with its list of numbers, and you can double-click on a name or number to dial it. The Log — Options menu allows you to specify what numbers are logged in terms of *outgoing*, *incoming* or *none*.

Note: The old Cardfile of Windows 3.1 had the considerable advantage of allowing much more than 9 numbers to be stores, and of using a note-card for each number.

Dial-up Networking

General: Dial-up Networking is provided with Windows 98, and this is a brief description for reference if you want to alter the settings. Dial-Up Networking allows you access to information on another computer even if your computer is not on a network. The remote computer that you are connecting to **must** be set up as a network server. Both computers must be equipped with modems and be running communications software. *Dial-up Networking* is mostly used for Internet connections.

Dial-up Networking

Setting up: To start the *Dial-Up Networking* setup wizard, click My Computer, and then click *Dial-Up Networking*. You will be asked for the contact number for the server computer. The connection will be established using the default name *My Connection* or a name that is programmed in by your Internet Provider. You can edit this later.

Editing a connection: Click *Dial-Up Networking* and place the cursor over the connection name. You can right-click to see a menu consisting of Connect, Create Shortcut, Delete, Rename and Properties. You can use *Rename* to change the name of the connection.

With the connection name selected, click Connections on the menu bar of Explorer. Click Settings item to change how your connection is handled. The first three options are *Show an icon on Taskbar when connected*, *Prompt for information before dialing* and *Show confirmation dialog after connection*. All of these are useful, particularly the first because it allows you to break the connection easily by double-clicking the icon and selecting the *Disconnect* option. You can opt for a *Redial* setting, and specify how many redials you will accept and what time should elapse between them if the number is engaged. The final options are whether or not to prompt use of *Dial-up Networking* when you are making a new connection.

Click File — Properties (or right-click on the name, and select Properties) to change items such as the telephone number, and details of protocols that both computers must use. You can also change your modem settings. Do not change other settings unless you have been advised to do so from the user of the remote computer.

Note: You are most likely to make use *of Dial-up Networking* when you are setting up an Internet connection. The settings will usually be configured automatically by the software that you obtain from the Information Provider.

Direct cable connection (DCC)

General: DCC is a simple piece of software that allows you to network two computers together. It is more commonly used to link a portable machine to a desktop computer, but can also be used to link two desktop machines or two portables. When DCC is running, one machine has access to the files and printer(s) of the other, and both machine can be used running other programs in other windows. A cable link is needed between the computers,

Setting up: You need to link the machines by a serial cable or a parallel cable. A serial cable is easier, because most computers will have a spare serial port, but if the serial link is too slow a Laplink parallel cable (which is **not** the same as a printer cable) can be used. You also need to have DCC installed on both computers. Use Control Panel — Add/Remove programs to add the Windows components for DCC (which also requires installing Dial-up Networking).

Use: Start DCC on both computers. Designate one computer as the host (whose files will be shared) and the other as the Guest (using the files of the Host). On the Host, use Explorer to mark the folders/files/printers that will be shared. For example, to share the whole of the C:\ drive (all folders) right-click on C:\ and then click on Sharing. You will see a form appear on which you must click on *Shared As* and fill in a reference name for the folder. You can then decide on the sharing options of *Read Only*, *Full* or *Depending on Password*. If you do not opt to share all of your hard drive you will need to assign sharing for the folders you want to make available. Printers are shared in the same way, right-clicking on the printer name and then on *Sharing*.

Note: This can be a very convenient way of ensuring that the desktop machine shares files with a portable, or using two desktop machines to hold more data than can be contained on one.

....

Disaster recovery

General: A disaster in this sense means that a fault in the hard drive will prevent Windows from loading, so that you have no access to the hard drive and so to the computer. It is for this type of situation that you are urged to make a *Startup* floppy when you install Windows 98.

Use: When the hard drive fails, insert the *Startup* floppy in the drive and restart. This will start the computer using MS-DOS, so that you need to have working knowledge of this system in order to recover use of your hard drive. This inevitably makes recovery a difficult matter for users who have only ever used Windows.

Once in DOS, you can type the command C:\ (press Enter/Return key) to see if access to the hard drive is possible. If the C:\> prompt message appears, the hard drive is working, and you can try using the DIR (Press Enter/Return key) command. If this shows a list of files, it should be possible to regain the use of the hard drive with data intact. Sometimes this can be done simply by using ScanDisk.

System Recovery: The system recovery that is available using the Startup disc now requires less knowledge of the workings of DOS and Windows, but can be used only if you have made a full system backup on tape or other suitable medium, using Microsoft Backup. You will need to have the Windows 98 CD-ROM in addition to the backup tape.

Recovery process: After starting the computer with the Startup floppy inserted, select *Start your computer with CD-ROM support from the Boot menu* (use arrow keys and

Windows 98 assistant

Enter/Return key to select). When you see the A:> prompt appear, type the command D: (assuming that your CD-ROM drive uses this letter) and then press the Enter/Return key.

When the A:> prompt returns, type:

CD TOOLS\SYSREC

–and press Enter/Return. When the A:> prompt returns, type:

PCRESTOR

–and press the Enter/Return key. Now follow the instructions that appear on the screen for reinstalling Windows 98.

System Recovery Wizard: After Windows 98 has been re-installed, the System Recovery Wizard starts. Click the *Next* box on the opening panel. Type, as requested, your name and (optionally) Company and click the *Next* button again. Click *Details* on the next panel. Start Help and read or print the whole of the Backup Help topic.

Click the *Close* button and then click the *Finish* button of the Wizard. Using Microsoft Backup, click *Restore backed up files*, and then follow the instructions for using your backup device. If your hardware has not changed, you can click the *Restore hardware settings* option, but if you have changed any hardware leave this option unused. You can now restore data files.

Creating a Startup disc: If you did not make a Startup disc when you installed Windows 98, or if you want another copy (highly recommended), proceed as follows. Start Control Panel, and click *Add/Remove Programs*. Click the *Startup Disk* tab and then click on *Create Disk* and follow the instructions that appear.

Note: Some BIOS types allow you to specify that the floppy will not be used for booting. If you have set this option, you will have to change this CMOS RAM setting before you can boot from the Startup floppy.

If you find that you cannot use your backup drive you will need to restore the driver. Click Start — Settings — Control Panel — System. Click *Device Manager*, double-click the backup device name, and click Driver. Click the *Update driver* button and follow the instructions that appear. You will be prompted to insert the driver software disc that came with the backup system.

If you use more than one computer, try all of this recovery routine on one spare machine so that you have some idea of what to expect when it has to be done in reality. You may never need the experience, but it would be daunting to have to try it out for the first time in a make-or-break context.

Disc cleanup

General: The Disc cleanup action is used to delete unwanted files so as to release more space on the hard drive. The files that are deleted are Internet cache files, temporary files of any kind, and program files that you have not used, or which belong to programs that have been deleted.

Starting: From Start, click in succession Programs — Accessories — System Tools — Disk Cleanup. The floppy drive will be checked before you see a panel that invites you to select a drive, with the C:\ hard drive offered as a default. Click the OK button to start the process. Another route is to right-click the drive name, click *Properties*, and then click the *Disk Cleanup* button.

Windows 98 assistant

You will see a list of files that have been detected for the cleanup process. You can click the *OK* button to remove these files, or use the *View Files* button for details.

More Options: The tab labelled *More Options* allows you to select Windows components and programs that you do not use and do not intend to use. In either case, you have to click the *Clean up* button and select these items for yourself. If you are using a hard drive that has not been converted to FAT 32 you can use this last option also, see the separate entry for **Drive converter**.

Settings: This tab has one setting only, to specify that if space is limited, Disk Cleanup will be run automatically. You can also run Disk Cleanup automatically by specifying it in the **Task Scheduler** (see separate entry).

Disc names

General: Each fixed drive or floppy disc can be named ('labelled') and the label name can be changed.

Method: Start My Computer by clicking on the icon. Click on the disc in the display that you want to rename, and then click File — Properties. Type the new name in the *Label* box, using up to 11 characters only. Click on the *OK* button to establish this new label name.

Notes: Names for drives or discs can be a useful reminder of your intentions. For example, if you use one hard drive for programs and another for data, using these names as labels will help to remind you when you see the drives listed in Explorer.

Disc space

General: The *File Manager* program of Windows 3.1 always reported free disc space along with file size of a selected file, but Explorer is not so convenient to use in this respect, though there are several ways of reporting disc space.

Methods: Start My Computer, maximise the window, and place the pointer on the name of a disc drive. The status-line display will show the number of Mbyte or Kbyte used, and the free space. The Explorer display will show disc free space when you click on a disc drive. If, however, you click on a filename to find the size of that file, you will no longer get the drive size when you click again on the drive unless you have clicked on another drive first. You may see the previous file size displayed instead.

You can get a more graphical display by clicking on any drive name with the right-hand mouse button and then clicking *Properties* in the menu. This will show a display of used and unused space for that drive. The same display is also available from the File — Properties menu of Explorer or of My Computer.

Notes: See also the details in the **My Computer** and **Explorer** entries.

Display

General: The *Display* item in Control Panel concerns the way that the monitor is used, and sets the Desktop appearance, as well as the resolution and colour range that can be used. Some *Display* items, such as *Desktop* are dealt with under separate entries, so that what follows concentrates on other aspects of the *Display* choices. Some options are specific to the type of monitor that you are using,

Windows 98 assistant

and the tabs example below shows the choices for the ADI MicroScan.

Tabs: Click the Control Panel item in Explorer or use Start — Settings — Control Panel. Click on *Display*. The tabs that appear are labelled *Background*, *Screen Saver*, *Appearance*, *Web*, *Effects* and *Settings*. You may also be able to obtain this display from an icon in the Taskbar. Depending on your monitor type you might not have all of these tabs available, or you might have others.

Background: See the entry for **Desktop**.

Screen Saver: A Screen Saver is a pattern that replaces the normal screen display when the display remains unchanged for a set time. The theory is that this avoids 'burning in' a display on the screen, an effect you can see on the monitors that display arrivals and departures at airports. In practice, unless you leave the computer switched on with an unchanging screen display for really long periods, you are not likely to see burn-in in the lifetime of the computer – most computers are used for only a couple of years before being replaced. Click on the *Screen Savers* tab to see what is available. The set contains:

(none)	3D Flower Box	3D Flying objects
3D Maze	3D Pipes	3D Text
Blank Screen	Channel Screen Saver	Curves and Colors
Flying Through Space	Flying Windows	Mystify Your Mind

Scrolling Marquee

The *Blank Screen* saver is rather worse than none at all, because it gives the impression that the computer has been

76

switched off, so that you should consider using any of the others.

You can opt for the screen-saver to be password protected, so that you can return to normal operation only by typing in a password. You can also specify how long the computer should remain idle before the screen saver is activated.

Settings: For many screen savers, the options obtained from the *Settings* button allow you to specify the object style, shading, colours, resolution and size. For the *Channel Screen Saver* you can go online to find a suitable Web page or Channel to use.

Energy saving: If your monitor features energy-saving modes, you can choose how long the computer can be idle before going into low-power standby, and how long before the monitor is completely shut off. These options will also be on the *Screen Saver* tab.

- Other screensavers can be bought, and are often given away as part of a set of software bundled with a magazine. Check that any screensaver you obtain in this way is suitable for Windows 98.

Appearance: See the entries for **Fonts, Icons** and **ToolTips**.

Settings: This tab allows you to alter the resolution and colour range of your display, assuming that the monitor type is capable. The *Color Palette* setting will be 16 colours for standard VGA, with options of 256 colours, *High Color* (16 bit) and *True Color* (24-bit or 30 bit). The two latter settings demand a fast video card with at least 2 Mbyte of memory, and a monitor to match. The *Fonts* setting is of *Large Fonts* or *Small Fonts* – use the *Small Fonts* settings for 640 × 480 resolution, and *Large Fonts* for higher resolution settings. You can also click the *Custom* button to set the font sizes for yourself from a ruler display that can be dragged to alter the number of pixels per inch. If you are using the higher-resolution settings, you can make the size of the displayed ruler match that of a real ruler held against the screen, ensuring that printed copy will be scaled to screen size. This may, however, cause some fonts to look much too small on a normal 14 inch monitor.

The resolution settings are altered by dragging a pointer over a scale labelled *Desktop Area*. The end of the scale marked *Less* will supply 640 × 480 resolution, VGA standard), and the end marked *More* will supply the maximum that your monitor can deliver, such as 800 × 600 or 1024 × 768. You can click a *Change Display* button to notify a change of monitor type and/or driver, but such changes are usually made when the **Add Hardware** action is being used.

The *Advanced* button on this tab will bring up another set of tabs whose names depend on the type of monitor. A typical set is *General*, *Adapter*, *Monitor*, *Performance* and *Color Management*, and you can also find *Panning*, *Color* and *Adjustment*. You seldom need to change the default settings of the options in these tabs.

Web: The *Web* tab of Display Properties allows you the options of viewing the Active Desktop as a Web page, and this is a default. A panel under this lists Web pages that can be used, with buttons marked *New*, *Delete*, *Properties* and *Reset All* affecting your choices. You can use the *New* button to browse for and install a new Web page, and the other actions affect a page selected from an existing list. These options are not particularly useful unless you work with a permanent Internet connection such as an ISDN line. You are not forced to use an active Web page if you opt for this type of Desktop appearance.

Effects: The main option in *Effects* is to *Hide icons when the desktop is viewed as a Web page*. This is a useful option if you do not make use of the Desktop, and if you like the Web page type of appearance.

The other options affect the appearance of icons with options of *Use large icons*, *Show icons using all possible colours*, *Animate windows*, *menus and lists*, *Smooth edges of screen fonts*, and *Show window contents while dragging*. The last item is a useful default, and the others can add to the appearance of your displays, though the animation option becomes tiring after some time.

Notes: The highest resolution settings are obtainable only if you are using a suitable monitor and driver, and unless you are changing only this aspect of your computer system you are stuck with the settings that were made when Windows 98 was installed.

Documents

General: A document, as far as Windows 98 is concerned, is a data file for a program, which might consist of text, of numbers, of graphics, sounds, or any mixture of these items. Windows 98 will keep a list of all suitable documents that have been opened, creating a shortcut so that you can quickly gain access to these documents again. Some older programs may create document types that do not appear in the list. You can open a document in its associated program by clicking on the document name in the Start — Documents list or in the Explorer list, see the entry for **association**.

Document list: Adding a document is automatic and there is no straightforward provision for cancelling this action. To empty the document list, click Start — Settings — Taskbar — Start Menu and click the button (in the lower Documents section) labelled *Clear*. You should clear the document list at frequent intervals.

Preview: You can preview any document provided that the *QuickView* program was installed with Windows 98. Click on the document name in Explorer, then on File — QuickView. If the *QuickView* item does not appear in the *File* menu, the item cannot be previewed, even if it has been associated with a program such as Notepad. You can, however, associate straightforward text files with *QuickView*, which is listed in the set of programs available for the **associate** action. See the **QuickView** entry for more details.

Send To: A document file can be sent to a floppy disc or to the printer by using Explorer. Start Explorer, select the document, and click File — Send To. This will display the choice of destinations, which can include networked drives. For more information, see the **Send To** entry.

Languages: The languages listed in the **country (regional) settings** entry are supported by Windows 98 automatically. If you want to work with documents that use languages originating in Central Europe, Greece, or Turkey, including Cyrillic or Baltic languages, you must install the multi-language support option. Close down all programs other than Explorer. Insert the Windows 98 CD-ROM or first floppy disc. Use *Control Panel* from the Start menu or from Explorer and click *Add/Remove Programs*. Select the *Windows Setup* tab, and click on *Multi-language Support*. Click the *Details* button to see the three support groups. The first deals with *Czech Republic*, *Hungarian*, *Polish and Slovenian*, the second with *Bulgarian*, *Belarusian and Russian*, and the third with *Greek*-based languages. Click on the OK button in each panel until the installation starts – if you install from floppies you will be prompted to insert the correctly numbered discs. You will be prompted to restart the computer so that the installation can be completed.

Icon: The icon for a document is determined by the type of document. In particular, if a document is associated with a program type, the icon for that type will be used. You may be able to change this icon as follows. From Explorer or My Computer, click View — Options and then click the *File Types* tab. Find the icon corresponding to the program that opens your document, and click the *Edit* button. The panel that appears contains the *Change Icon* option and you will usually find one or more optional icons available. Click on the icon you want to use (you can click on the *Default* button to restore the original icon). If you want to look through a larger list of icons, click the *Browse* button, and look for the file called MORICONS.DLL in the Windows folder. You can select an icon from the (large) set that appears.

Downloading

When you download a Web page, only that page is visible and is available on your computer. When you press a hyperlink button (usually underlined or coloured), a new page or set of pages will be downloaded. You can save the current page, but if you look at it again when you are offline you cannot use the hyperlinks that you did not use when you were online, so that clicking the buttons will **not** produce the other pages unless you have downloaded and saved them also. Graphics on a page are also not saved along with the page.

Saving current page: With the page on screen, click File — Save A File. On the display that appears, click the folder into which you want to place the page file. Type the name in the *File Name* box and click the *Save* button.

Windows 98 assistant

Saving linked pages: You can save a linked page after opening it, using the method above. Alternatively, you can save a linked page without opening it. Click the hyperlink that downloads the page with the **right-hand** mouse button, and then click on *Save Target As*, and supply a destination and filename, then click on *Save*.

Drive converter (FAT32)

General: When a file or folder is stored on the hard drive, it is allocated reference numbers which are stored in a file allocation table (FAT). MS-DOS and earlier versions of Windows use a 16-bit number system, which restricts the number of FAT entries to 65536. This was adequate when hard drives were of around 40 Mbyte capacity, but large hard drives could be catered for only by storing units, called clusters, that might be of up to 32 Kbyte in size. This led to a considerable waste of space on the drive, because a cluster would be allocated even if only a few bytes needed to be stored.

In Windows 3.1 and Windows 95, the use of the *DriveSpace* system eliminated this waste by storing data in one single large file, making use of complete clusters with only one cluster unfilled. The penalty for this more efficient use of space was slower operation because of the need to code the data in a more compact way. This system fell out of use when hard drive prices dropped, and though it can still be used with Windows 98, it is preferable not to use it. Drivespace has not been featured in this book.

FAT32: Smaller clusters can be used if the FAT uses large numbers, so that Windows 98 features a 32-bit number system. This is not compatible with a drive that was formatted with the older versions of Windows 95, and if you are using such a drive you will be given the option to change to the new FAT32 system. If you bought a computer in mid-1997 or later, it is very likely that it uses a later version of Windows 95 (the OSR2 version, which is very similar to Windows 98) that utilises the FAT32 system.

Checking: To check the file system that your computer uses, click on My Computer, and right-click on your hard drive description. From the menu that appears, click *Properties*. The pane that appears should show the file system as FAT32 if the drive has been formatted in this way.

Converting hard drive: If your drive is formatted using the older FAT system, you can convert it to FAT32 by running the Drive Converter program. You need to know that you cannot easily reverse this process, that you cannot use some older disc utilities or older versions of Windows, and that removable discs can be converted but can then be used only on machines that run the FAT32 system.

To run the converter, Click Start, and then Programs — Accessories — System Tools — Drive Converter. You can also get to Drive Converter through the Disk Cleanup panel.

Checking: You can check which system is in use by clicking with the right-hand mouse button on the hard drive name or icon in Explorer. Click *Properties*, and look for the name that appears next to the title *File System*.

Note: If you bought a computer in 1997 that was fitted with the later version of Windows 95 then your hard drive will already use FAT32 and the Drive Converter options will be greyed out. It is also unavailable for small hard drives.

Drives

General: A modern computer can be expected to provide a hard drive, a floppy drive (which may be one of the 120 Mbyte type) and a CD-ROM drive, all as standard fittings. A tape (streamer) drive may be present, or a CD R/W drive (read/write) used in place of, or along with, the CD-ROM type.

Large hard drives: Windows 98 allows you to use hard drives of capacity up to 2 TB (terabytes), which is 2048 Gbyte. This does not entail the wasteful use of the drives that was caused by 16-bit file allocation tables (FAT). Windows now uses a 32-bit FAT, allowing the clusters on the hard drive to be much smaller. This change was first implemented in Windows 95 in the (UK) 1997 versions available then only to manufacturers. See entry for **Drive Converter**.

Shut down: IDE hard drives can be configured to shut down when not in use, conserving power and drive life. Note that this does not apply to SCSI drives, only to IDE or EIDE types, and all IDE drives are equally affected — you cannot opt to shut down one drive by itself.

Click Control Panel — Power Management. The Power Schemes tab contains the *Power Schemes* box that can be set for *Always On*, *Home/Office desk*, or *Portable/Laptop*. Select whichever best applies to your computer, using *Always On* if you don't want to use any type of scheme. The lower part of the panel shows the *Turn off hard discs* box, and you can click the arrowhead to specify the time of inactivity that is allowed before the hard drive is closed down. Pressing a key or moving the mouse will restore the hard drive actions after a short time.

Note that if you have not installed energy-saving features for a portable computer, the options will not appear on the Power Management tabs.

Checking for errors, see **ScanDisk**.

Defragmenting, see separate entry.

Changing letter: Drive letters are normally assigned by Windows when a drive is installed or when Windows is installed. You may be able to change a drive letter if you need to by using Control Panel — System — Device Manager and clicking the [+] sign next to the drive type, then clicking the drive name. Click the *Settings* tab, and look for a drive letter. If no drive letter appears or if the drive letter is greyed out you cannot change the letter.

DVD-ROM

General: DVD means digital versatile disc, a development of CD that can store much larger amounts of data and transfer it more rapidly. The versatility that forms part of the name arises because the DVD can be used for computer data, music or video. A DVD can be single-sided, single layer, storing 4.7 Gbyte as compared to the 650 Mbyte of CD, and the double-sided two-layer version of DVD can store 17 Gbyte. Like CDs, DVD can be obtained as read-only, write-once (DVD-R), or DVD-RAM (read/write). DVD sound and video players are already available as attachments to TV receivers and Hi-Fi systems.

Windows 98 support: Windows 98 supports the use of several makes of DVD drives. This allows you to use video playback of discs to your TV receiver if you have the DVD decoder card and suitable software for a PAL type of TV display. DVD drives for the PC can be expected soon.

Edit menu, Explorer

General: This is the usual type of *Edit* menu on both versions of Explorer, providing for the *Cut, Copy* and *Paste* actions, but with *Select All* and *Find* actions also. Windows Explorer adds *Page* and *Invert Selection* items, and Internet

Windows 98 assistant

Explorer has *Paste Shortcut* and *Find* items. In the lists that follow IE means Internet Explorer and WE means Windows Explorer.

The Cut, Copy and Paste actions are used normally with Windows Explorer, but these items in Internet Explorer are intended for use when you are viewing the source code for a page, or creating a page of your own, and they have limited uses on a normal Web page display.

Cut (IE): Will cut the selected text in a *source-code* page (click View — Source). The *Cut* action looks as if it is supported on a normal Web page display, but the selected text is not cut. Shortcut is Ctrl-X. Cut (WE) will cut selected files.

Copy(IE): Allows you to use the copy action on either a normal Web page or its corresponding source code (use View — Source). Selected text can be copied to other documents using this action. Shortcut is Ctrl-C. Copy (WE) will copy selected files.

Page(IE): Allows you to work with Web pages in Front Page Express, a utility for Web page editing. This is not covered in this book. BP441 *Creating Web Pages using Microsoft Office 97* is a good introduction to Web page design, and you should also consult BP433 *Your Own Web Site on the Internet*.

Paste(IE): Will paste material from the clipboard into a source-code page only, not into a normal Web page display. Shortcut is Ctrl-V. Paste (WE) will paste cut or copied files to a the current location.

Select All: Can be used in IE to select all of a Web page or its corresponding source file. In WE, select a set of files, so that all of the text can be copied and pasted to another document. Shortcut is Ctrl-A.

Find (on this page): Will find a word or phrase that you type into the Find box. You can click option boxes for *Start from Top* and *Match case*. The *Find* action is for the downloaded page only, and does not find other items on the Internet. Shortcut is Ctrl-F.

Editors (HTML)

General: A page in the HTML system is constructed from a set of statements, the form of which will be recognisable to anyone who has used a programming language such as BASIC. Any page can be edited by editing the HTML file, and you can view such a file without editing it if you are curious about the system. You do not need to be able to master the HTML language in order to create your own Web pages, because you can buy HTML editors that will create a page from your instructions. You can create HTML pages using Word 97 (see BP411), or by using the *Front Page Express* utility of Windows 98.

Editing: With the page loaded, click View — Source. An alternative is to click on the page using the **right-hand** mouse button, and then click on *View Source* in the menu that appears. This will open the Notepad editor of Windows with the HTML source file loaded. You can save this file to another folder for further editing if you prefer not to change the existing file.

Explorer

General: Explorer is the Windows 98 drive, folder, file and Internet management program, and it exists in separate forms called Windows Explorer and Internet Explorer. The two are not totally identical, and though you can for most of your computing time work with just Windows Explorer

Windows 98 assistant

(which allows Web access), you need to open the appropriate version if you want to alter Internet Options or File Options. There is a way around this, detailed later.

Using Windows Explorer you can view contents of disc drives and folders, copy and move files, check properties of all items (from drives to files) and operate the Control Panel and the Recycle Bin. You also have full access to Internet sites.

Starting: Click the *Start* button, followed by Programs — Windows Explorer. If Explorer is running when you quit Windows, it will be restarted the next time you switch on your computer – there is no need to keep a shortcut to Explorer in the *Startup* folder. You can use the same sequence to open Internet Explorer, but you would not normally use both programs together.

Display: The default Explorer display consists of an Explorer bar on the left hand side which for Windows Explorer normally carries a list of drives and folders. This can be changed to show the type of lists (Search, Channels, History, Favorites) that appear in the Internet Explorer.

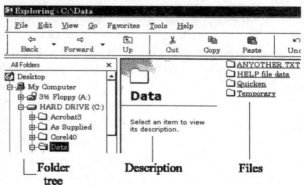

The right hand side of the screen contains a folder/files list or a Web page content. The boundary can be dragged to left or right as you prefer. In Windows Explorer you can opt to see a central strip, illustrated here, that shows explanations of files in a folder.

The Windows Explorer *All Folders* tree diagram starts with Desktop and My Computer and displays the drives (hard, floppy, and CD-ROM), the Control Panel, Printer and Recycle Bin. You can remove the left-hand display by clicking on the × icon at its top right-hand corner. You can replace the display using View — Explorer bar — All folders. Other options in this menu allow you to display the Internet Explorer options.

Tree display (WE): The tree display at the left hand side shows each section of the Explorer tree as a list of drives and main folders, and a box with a [+] sign indicates that further information is available by clicking the box. For example, clicking the box for a hard drive will result in expanding the tree diagram to show the folders of the hard drive, with a corresponding display of folders and files in the right-hand side. Click again on the box to collapse the tree again. In this way you can see as much detail as you want — this is particularly useful if you use more than one hard drive, or a drive which has been partitioned into two or more parts. You can also select a drive and press the asterisk key (*) on the numeric keypad — this will have the effect of opening out all folders, equivalent to clicking on each [+] sign in the folders for that drive. You can also double-click a folder to open out a display of its sub-folders.

Files and Folders display: The display of folders and files on the right-hand side of the Windows Explorer window can be tailored to your requirements by using the View menu. You can opt for a Web page type of display by ticking this option. You can opt for a set of icons only by clicking on *Large Icons* or *Small Icons*. The other options produce lists, and the *List* option shows much the same set of icons and names as the *Small Icons* set, but with the arrangement sorted vertically into columns rather than horizontally into rows. The *Details* option is particularly useful, because it shows *Size*, *Type* and *Modification Date* for all files. The *Line Up Icons* action is available only if the *Large Icons* or *Small Icons* display is in use.

Icons can be arranged in order, and an *Autoarrange* option is available if you have selected *Large Icons* or *Small Icons*. All arrangements show folders sorted ahead of files. The other arrangements, which are also available when you select a list, are to sort in order of *Name*, *Type*, *Size* and *Date*. The *Name* arrangement sorts into alphabetical order of main filename, and the *Type* order sorts in order of extension letters. The *Size* and *Date* options are particularly useful if you want to find very large or very small files, or to find your oldest or newest files. A sort arrangement will remain in place until you cancel it.

Folder Options (WE): The View — Folder options — General menu allows you to choose how you will see your Windows Explorer display. The default is *Web style*, making Windows Explorer and Internet Explorer look almost identical. You can also opt to use *Classic style*, so that your Windows Explorer displays look much the same as they did in Windows 95. The third option is *Custom*, allowing you to determine for yourself how files and folders are displayed and used. If you use Custom, the *Settings* button shows what choices you have, which are for *Active desktop*, *Browse folders*, *View Web content in folders* and Click items.

The Active desktop can use the classic (Windows 95) type of display or the Web style. Browse folders can be done by opening each folder in the same window or by using a new window for each folder. *Viewing Web content* can be used for all folders with HTML content or only for folders selected as being viewed as a Web page. Clicking can be specified as single-click, with an underline appearing optionally when an item is pointed at, or at all times. You can also opt for the older style of double-clicking if you cannot get on with single-click actions (which are much easier once you become accustomed to them).

Once you have made your choice (default is Web style) you can click the View tab. The button *Like current folder* can be clicked to make all file and folder views the same as the current view, so allowing you to choose your preferred options and impose them on all views. The other button is marked *Reset all folders* so that you can use a different type of View for different selected folders.

The settings for view start with seven selection boxes. The first is *Remember each folder's View settings*, and you can tick this to ensure that the same settings will always be used for a particular folder. This allows you to alter a view of a folder and always see it with these alterations, as distinct from imposing the same settings on all displays. Click on the box marked *Display the Full Path in Title Bar* if you want to see the full path for your files – this is useful if you are going to start an MS-DOS program. The third box is labelled *Hide File Extension for known File Types*. This shows the main filenames only, and makes for a less-cluttered display, providing that you remember the icon shapes for different file types.

The box marked *Show Map Network Drive button on Toolbar* is relevant only if you are connected to a network. The box marked *Show File attributes in Detail view* is useful if you need to know more about the files in some folders, but this extra information applies only to a *Details* view, not to the default icon or list views.

The next box is labelled *Show pop up Description for folder and desktop items*, and ticking this box will ensure that you see a description of a file or folder when the pointer is over it. This is not needed if you have used the option to *View as Web Page* (*View* menu), because this information appears in such a View. The last check box is for *Allow all uppercase names*, which can be ticked to prevent the default changing of names into lowercase.

These selection boxes are followed by a set of three options for the display of Hidden and System files. Your options are:

Do not show hidden or system files
Do not show hidden files
Show all files

and the first choice is useful as a way of preventing you from deleting important files.

The last part of the View options is titled *Visual Settings* and consists of three check-box items:

Hide icons when Desktop is viewed as Web page
Smooth edges of screen fonts
Show window contents while dragging

The *Desktop* icons might as well be hidden if you make no use of them, and the other two choices are also useful. Note that some of these last options are available in the Display options also.

Copy and Move: These Windows Explorer actions are most easily carried out by dragging. The default action is that dragging a file between folders on the same hard (or floppy) drive is **always** a move action, but dragging between two different drives (such as floppy disc and hard drive folder) is **always** a copy action. Select the file or folder to be copied or moved and drag it to the new position. The alternative to dragging is to use the *Edit* commands of *Cut*, *Copy* and *Paste*.

- If you want to enforce a copy action in a drag between folders on the same drive, hold down the Ctrl key when you start a drag action. If you want to enforce a move action between the hard drive and a floppy, hold down the Shift key when you start a drag action.

- If the destination for your drag action is not in view, drag to the top or the bottom of the Directories display panel so that this part of the display scrolls. It is easier to locate your target folder if you ensure that it is visible before you start dragging.

Rename: To rename a folder that uses the single-click action, right-click on the name and on the menu that appears, click *Rename*. A frame will appear around the name, and you can delete the name and type another. Alternatively, you can use the cursor arrow keys to delete part of a name and then retype a portion. Press the RETURN key, or click somewhere else, to establish the new filename.

New file/folder: With a drive or folder selected, click on File — New and when the options appear, on *File* or *Folder* (or on any of the specified types that are listed). The new file or folder will appear in a drive or folder listing, with a default name ready to edit so that you can type in whatever name you want to use (then press the RETURN key or click elsewhere).

Run program: Click on a program name to start it running. If the program is an MS-DOS type, it will run in an MS-DOS window, see later. If you click on a document filename which is associated with a program, the program will start with the document opened. You can also use the File — Open menu item.

Refresh display: When files have been added to a folder by other methods (that is, not using Explorer) the Explorer display can be updated either by pressing the F5 key or by using the View — Refresh menu action.

Windows 98 assistant

Properties: The *Properties* of Folders or Files can be changed using the Windows Explorer display. Click on a file or folder with the right-hand mouse button and select *Properties*, or select the file or folder, and click File — Properties. For a folder you will see a single panel containing entries for *Type*, *Location*, *Size* and *Contains*. The *MS-DOS File Name* will appear, with, if appropriate, a *Created* date. The attributes of *Read-only*, *Hidden*, *Archive* and *System* will appear as boxes that are ticked if the attribute is set. The *System* box is greyed out to prevent alteration.

The display for files can be more complex. In general, document files and some *types* of program files use only the same *General* panel as is used for folders, but many document files, particularly from Word, also contain tabs marked *Summary* and *Statistics* that provide additional information on the contents of the file.

Some program files, and in particular, MS-DOS program files, use up to six tabs. Programs that run under Windows have a *Version Tab* on their *Properties* set. This shows information on the use of the file, and has an information list with headings of *Company Name*, *Internal Name*, *Language*, *Original Filename*, *Product Name* and *Product Version*. Click on a name to see the related information. The *Product Name* information can sometimes be a useful way of finding if a file is needed – you may find, for example, that it is used as part of a set that you do not need.

For the MS-DOS program set, which can be ignored if you do not use MS-DOS programs, see the **MS-DOS** entry.

Shortcuts: You can create a shortcut to a file by dragging it to a new location with the Ctrl and Shift keys both held down. Alternatively, you can drag with the right-hand mouse button held down and select *Shortcut Here* from the menu that appears when you release the button over the destination folder (the other options are *Copy* and *Cancel*).

Menu items: The Windows Explorer menus provide some alternatives to actions that can be carried out faster using the mouse, and some actions that cannot be carried out using the mouse. The contents of the File menu will depend on whether you have selected a folder or a file (and depend also on the file type).

For a document file, the typical *File* menu content would be *Open*, *Print, New* (file) *QuickView*, *Send To*, *New* (folder, shortcut, etc.), *Create Shortcut*, *Delete*, *Rename*, *Properties, Work Offline* (in a Web view) and *Close*. There will be a list of recently used folders/files between the *Properties* and *Work Offline* items and you can select any of these with a single click. The *QuickView*, *Send To*, and *New* (file) items are separate entries in their own right in this book, and there are faster options for the other actions. If you have selected a document file which has no association, the *Open* item will become *Open With* so that you can select a program to use in opening the file. The *File* menu also contains the other *New*, which will create a new folder or a new shortcut. If you use Microsoft Office, the *New* list will also show a selection of Office document types.

In the *Edit* menu, the *Undo* action can be used to reverse some step, such as deletion or renaming, that you have had second thoughts about. The type of action (*Undo Delete*, *Undo Rename*) is specified. The menu options of *Cut*, *Copy* and *Paste* are also contained here with reminders of their key options of Ctrl-X, Ctrl-C and Ctrl-V respectively. The *Paste Shortcut* item is used when you have copied or cut a shortcut from another location and you want to place the shortcut into the current folder. Two particularly useful commands are *Select All*, which will select all the files in the current folder, and *Invert Selection* which will deselect all the selected files in a folder and select the files which were not previously selected.

The *Tools* menu contains *Find* which has an entry of its own in this book, and also the Network mapping options which do not apply to a solo user of a computer.

Notes: Explorer is very versatile, and you should keep it available each time you start Windows by ensuring that it is running when you quit Windows. Once you have found a favourite *View* and imposed it on all folders, you can try experimenting with other views on selected folders.

See the entry for Internet Explorer for the use of Explorer as a browser, and for the Internet Options. This also shows the use of the browser as a Windows Explorer.

Favourites

General: Explorer, like Microsoft Word, maintains a *Favorite Files* folder, and if you also have Word on your hard drive, this folder will be shared between Word and both varieties of Explorer. The use of this folder is a fast way to find a small set of files and folders that you often use, and any Web page that is displayed on Internet Explorer can be saved to this folder or a sub-folder, if you want rapid access to it.

Saving Web page: With the page displayed, click Favorites — Add to Favorites and click on the *OK* button. Another option is to click with the **right-hand** mouse button over the page and then select *Add to Favorites* from the menu that appears. You can click the *Create in >>* button if you want to add the page to a sub-folder of Favourites such as *Net*.

Favourites folder: You can, if you wish, change the filename that is displayed, or opt to save it in a different folder. If you use Word, it is useful to take the *Create New*

Folder option of this Explorer panel, because it allows you to name a sub-folder of *Favorites* which can be used exclusively for Internet (or Word) pages. The contents of this folder can be viewed when you click on the *Favorites* menu item of Internet Explorer and then on the arrowhead at the sub-folder filename. This avoids confusion between the contents of the *Favorites* folder of Word and the section used for Internet Explorer. If you do this, you must use the *Organise Favorites* menu option each time you add a page to your favourites.

Open: To open a favourite Web page, click on the Favourites icon and select the page from the display that appears

Shortcut option: An alternative to the use of the favourites folder is the use of a shortcut. with the page displayed, click File — Create Shortcut. A message will appear to notify you that the shortcut will be placed on the Desktop — click the *OK* button to complete the action. If you minimize or reduce all open windows, you can then drag the shortcut to any other place, such as a folder displayed in Windows Explorer.

Note: You can also opt to show *Favorites* on the left-hand bar of the Explorer display. Click View — Explorer bar — Favorites to do this.

File menu, IE

General: The File menu of Internet Explorer is smaller than that of Windows Explorer and is used mainly for the Open and Save commands, and also for printing and page setup for Web pages. It also contains the important *Work offline* option to save you from running up an excessive telephone bill by allowing you view downloaded information offline.

Windows 98 assistant

New: Leads to a choice of *Window*, or of *Message*, *Post*, and *Contact*. Depending on your use of IE you may also see *Appointment*, *Meeting Request*, *Task*, *Task Request*, *Journal*, *Note* or *Internet call*. *Window* is used to launch another complete copy of Internet Explorer, not simply another window for Web pages. You can switch from one copy to the other using the Taskbar or the Alt-Tab keys as usual. Shortcut is Ctrl-N. The other normal options are for creating a new mail message, post a new message to a newsgroup, or enter a new name and e-mail; in your *Address book*.

Open: Will provide a panel into which you can type a full Internet address if you are connected online. Shortcut is Ctrl-O. A *Browse* button allows you to search for files that you have saved, with the default of looking for HTML files. You can also opt to find files of types TXT, GIF, JPEG, PNG, ART, AU, AIFF, XBM, or for a display of *All Files*. Note that this is a convenient way of reading saved HTML files. You can also type a Web address directly into the Address space if you have opted to have this visible.

Save: Can be used only if you have a page with an established filename, otherwise use *Save As*. The *Save* option is greyed out unless you have altered the page. Shortcut is Ctrl-S.

Save As: Allows you to save a Web page as a (local) file on your hard drive. This is useful for some files that consist mainly of text and which contain information you are likely to need often. Note that picture content of Web pages is **not** saved by this command. To save a picture or any other hyperlink, you need to click the hyperlink with the right-hand mouse button and then click *Save Target As*.

Page Setup: Is used when you want to print Web pages so that you can specify the paper you will use in your printer. When you click this option, you will see an image of a page, and you can set *Paper Size, Paper Source, Orientation* (*Portrait* or *Landscape*), and the margins for top, bottom, left and right. You can also specify a header and/or footer, and set up the printer. The page image will display the effects of the changes that you make.

* You might find that footers on a Web page are slightly cut off. You can increase the bottom margin to counteract this.

Print: Will print the current Web page or other document that IE is using, using the dimensions that you have specified in *Page Setup*. The shortcut is Ctrl-P.

Send: Will send the selected file using the options of *Page by Email*, *Link by Email*, or *Shortcut to Desktop*.

Properties: Can be clicked to see information on the current Web page. The Properties panel contains the *General* tab which shows entries for *Protocol*, *Type* and *Address*, of which the latter is the only useful entry for most viewers. The size and dates of creation and modification for the file are also shown.

Current file: a set of current files/pages are shown in a panel following the *Properties* item. You can click on any item to use it.

Work offline: can be ticked to prevent Explorer from automatically going online to extract information. Stored information can be viewed as if it were online, and if information requires connection you will be warned by a message so that you can decide whether or not to stay offline.

The amount of information that you can see offline depends on your settings for retaining Temporary and History files, and you may find that only a few pictures are retained.

Close: Will close down Internet Explorer.

Filenames

General: Windows 98, like Windows 95, supports the use of long filenames. In theory, a filename of up to 255 characters can be used, but this includes all the characters in the file path (including intermediate folders). A filename can include spaces and can use upper or lower case letters.

When needed: You will be asked to supply a filename when you use the *Save As* command in any application. The filename can include an extension, a set of up to three letters placed following a full-stop at the end of a name. Many applications packages will put in an extension automatically, so that if you use Word to save a document and supply the name **This is my first.doc** this will be saved using the doc extension as **This is my first doc.doc.**

Older applications: Older applications can deal only with the MS-DOS type of filename that used up to eight characters in the main name, with no spaces allowed. When you supply a filename for such an application you **must** conform to these older specifications. If you open a file in such an application, you will see any long filenames compressed to the eight-character format. This is done by using the characters ~1 at the end of the name and keeping the first six relevant characters of the name that was used (spaces are not used). For example, if the file was called howaboutthisname it will be renamed as howabo~1. The number can be changed to accommodate filenames which have the same first six characters.

File types

General: Each program that you have installed will create or use data files, and the extension letters for these files describe the type of file (such as DOC for Word text, or

TXT for ASCII files). When you install a new program, its file types will be added to the list that Windows keeps, but if you simply import some data files from a floppy this addition to the types list does not take place. You can add the files, using methods that are used for association.

Adding a new file type: Starting in Windows Explorer or My Computer, click View — Folder options — File Types, you will see a list of registered file types. Click on any file type to see the extension letters of the data file and the program that can be used to open the file. Click on the *New Type* button. Click in the *Description of Type* box and type a brief description – this will appear in Explorer if you have specified to see details of files. Click in the *Associated Extension* box and type the extension letters that your new file type uses.

You can then specify what actions you require, usually *Open* and *Print*. Click the *New* button to see the *New Action* panel. Type the action (such as *Open*) and, in the *Application* space, specify the program that will carry out this action. For example, to open a BMP file you could specify Paint. Use the *Browse* button to find the program you want to use and click the *Open* button to establish this as the required program. There is a box marked *Use DDE* which can be ticked if the program manual advises you to do so.

When you return to the main panel your action will appear entered, and you can click the *Use QuickView* box if you want to be able to use *QuickView* on this type of file.

Remove file type: Click on the file type in the View — Options — File Types display. You will be reminded that removing the file from the list will make it inaccessible by clicking. The list usually contains a large number of files that you would not normally start in that way.

Windows 98 assistant

Change Icon: You can click the *Change Icon* button in the *View Types* list to see the range of icons that are available. For a new file, you can choose from a set contained in a file called SHELL32.DLL which is contained in the folder C:\WINDOWS\SYSTEM. You can also use the *Browse* button to use another icon file, such as the icons file C:\WINDOWS\MORICONS.DLL. Click on an icon to use it as the icon for the selected file type.

Notes: While using the *Edit* option, you can click the box marked *Always Show Extension* to ensure that this file type is always shown with its extension letters even if you have opted not to show the extension letters of files.

Find

General: The Find action is available from the *Start* button menu or from the *File* menu of My Computer or Windows Explorer when a drive has been selected. Any file or folder that exists on a hard drive, or on a CD-ROM or floppy that has been inserted, can be found, and search conditions can be typed and saved if a similar search is likely to be wanted again. Files that have been deleted (to the Recycle Bin) can be found and retrieved provided that the Bin has not been emptied. The Find action can also extend to other computers on a network, files on the Internet and *People* who have an e-mail or Web address.

Starting Find: From Explorer, click Tools — Find — Files or Folders. From My Computer, click File — Find. From the Start button, click Find — Files or Folders.

Specifying a search: When Find starts, you will see the three-part specification panel, but for many types of searches you need only the *Name and Location* Panel. More elaborate searches are needed if you are working on a network. Fill in the filename, or part of the filename that you are looking for in the *Named* box. If you know only part of a name, represent the rest with one or more asterisks. For example, you can type IAN*.DOC if you know only the first three letters and the extension, or MOR*.* if you know the first three letters only. Click the arrowhead to see some items that have been used in previous searches.

The *Look In* section is used to specify the search area. If you have absolutely no idea where the file/folder might be located, use My Computer in *Look In*. This will ensure that all drives are searched, and is particularly useful if you have more than one hard drive, or a partitioned drive, with data in all portions. If, however, you know that the type of file you are looking for is in one particular drive you can save time by specifying this, such as D:\. You may even be able to select a folder that you feel certain contains the file you want to find. Always ensure that the box marked *Include Subfolders* is ticked. If you are looking for a file on the Net, use the Start button *Find* options.

- You can click the arrowhead in the *Look In* portion to see other locations, and you can use the *Browse* button to find a specific folder to search.

When you have specified your file as closely as you can, click the *Find Now* button to carry out the search. The results, showing file paths, will appear in a window that opens up beneath the *Find* panel. The *View* menu options can be used (in the same way as in Explorer) to determine how the files are displayed.

Options: A search is more difficult if no part of the filename can be recalled. The *Date* section of *Find* allows you to specify by date. The default option is *All Files*, but you can alter this by clicking on *Find All Files Modified, Created or Last Accessed* allowing you to specify a range of dates in the

Between option, or a prior time using *During the Previous Months* or *During the Previous Days*.

The *Advanced* panel allows you to specify registered file types (see the file type entry). The default is *All Files and Folders*, but you can click the arrowhead to select any file type that is registered in your copy of Windows. If you know (roughly) the size of the file, you can opt for the *Size Is* box, clicking to select *At Least* or *At Most*, and using the twin arrowheads to fill in a size in Kbyte.

Menus: The File menu of Find contains, after a search has been carried out, *Create Shortcut*, *Delete*, *Rename*, *Properties*, *Open Containing Folder*, *Save Search* and *Close*. If no search has been carried out, only the last two of the items are available.

The *Edit* menu consists of *Undo*, *Cut*, *Copy*, *Select All* and *Invert Selection*, all corresponding to the commands in Explorer. The *View* menu is the same as that of Explorer. The *Options* menu contains *Case Sensitive* which is useful if a filename contains both lowercase and uppercase letters, and the *Save Results* option.

Notes: When a search has been carried out, you can clear it by clicking the *New Search* button. This will clear the results of the previous search, and you can then click *Find Now* to start a new search with new criteria.

Find action IE

General: The IE Find action can refer to searching for text in a file that is currently held in your computer, or searching the Internet for information. The first type of Find is simple, the second depends on what search programs you can download and use.

Text on a page: With the page on screen, click Edit — Find (on this page), and fill in the text that you want to find in the form that appears. You can use the options of *Start from top of page*, and/or *Match case*.

Internet search: Click the *Search* icon on the Toolbar, or use the Go — Search the Web menu item. The default action is to download the Microsoft search home page: http://home.microsoft.com/access/allinone.asp. See under **Browsing the Internet** for further information.

Floppy discs

General: The floppy disc is still the primary backup method for data files, and the main distribution method for software, despite its limited capacity, though floppy discs of 100–120 Mbyte capacity are available and supported by Windows 98 A new driver for floppy discs has been designed, and provides faster operation.

Use: The floppy drive appears as an icon in the My Computer and Explorer displays. You can copy a file from any hard drive folder to the floppy by dragging it to the floppy disc icon. With the floppy drive selected, click the File — Properties item to check the state of the disc (used and unused space) and to activate tools for checking disc surface.

Format: To format a new disc open My Computer, select the floppy drive, and use File — Format. This opens a panel that starts with the capacity figure that is, by default, 1.4 Mbyte, and you would normally format all discs to this figure (see note below). The Format options are *Quick*, which is suitable for reformatting a disc that has been previously formatted and used, *Full*, for a new disc or one that has been formatted to a different size, and *Copy System*

Windows 98 assistant

Files only, used for a formatted disc to be used as an MS-DOS system disc (see also **Startup Disc** entry).

The other options are to type in a label name (no more than 11 characters), to specify that *No Label* name will be used, to *Display Summary when Finished* and to *Copy System Files Only*.

Copy disc: A floppy disc can be copied to another floppy in one action even if the computer contains only one floppy drive, and this action is important if you want to make backups of your original distribution discs for important programs. To copy a disc, put the disc that contains the files in the drive, and click My Computer. Select the drive, and click on File — Copy Disk. You will see a panel that contains two sections, both labelled with the letter for the floppy drive (usually A:). When the progress indicator reached half-way you will be prompted to place a blank formatted disc into the drive to complete the copying action.

- You can continue using the computer while copying is going on, but there is a risk that when the *Change disk* notice appears you may press a key that starts the copy to the disc that is already in the drive.

Installing from: To install a new Windows 98 program from the floppy drive, you should unless advised otherwise use the Control Panel and click *Add/Remove Programs*. Place the first (or only) disc into the drive. Click the *Install* key, and unless the A: drive is automatically used, specify this drive. The action will search for a file called INSTALL or SETUP and display it, so that you can start the installation. If more than one disc is used in a set, you will be prompted to replace discs as the installation proceeds.

Installing a modern Windows 98 program in this way will allow the program to be removed (uninstalled) later, provided that no files are deleted manually. Many older programs carry on their disc labels the instructions to insert the disc in the drive, click Start — Run and type a name such as A:\INSTALL or A:\SETUP. The *Add/Remove Programs* method can be used for these discs, but it will not be possible to remove the program later except by manual methods (locating the files and deleting them).

Notes: You can use the File — Create Shortcut menu item of My Computer, with the floppy drive selected, to place a shortcut to the floppy drive on the Desktop.

Use Control Panel to speed up floppy drive use. Click Setup and then Performance, followed by File System. Click the *Removable disk* tab and click *Enable write-behind caching on all removable disk drives*. Make sure that in the *Floppy disk* tab, the box marked *Search for new floppy disk drives each time your computer starts* is **cleared**.

Large-capacity floppy drives may look attractively-priced, but the availability of CD-RW drives (which will write CDs either in ROM form or in re-writeable form) allows the use of much cheaper media (about £1 for a write once disc, around £15 for a rewriteable type). The costs of the rewriteable discs are expected to drop rapidly, but prices of 100 Mbyte floppies are being maintained at the time of writing. Tape is by far a better medium for archiving large amounts of data at low cost.

Folders

General: A folder is the name for a collection of files, formerly called a *directory*. Clicking on a folder will display the files that it contains.

Style: The classic style of folder display is of names on the left side of Windows Explorer and files on the right, with files displayed as icons or name lists. You can opt to display folders as Web pages, and to use the settings of the current folder for all folders.

Use Explorer View — Folder options to see the three-tab display, with the *General* tab showing. If you opt for *Web style* your folders will be displayed as Web pages, and selection is automatic when the pointer is over a folder or filename. Only a single click is needed to open a file (open document or run program), and folder and file names appear underlined in the right-hand section of Explorer, with a central section used for comments. This is the style that is the default and is illustrated in this book. You can also opt for the older Windows 95 (classic) style, or you can use the Custom option to create your own style.

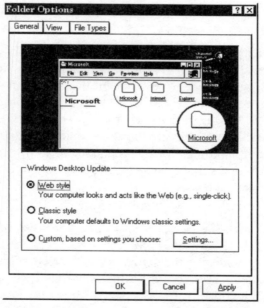

Folder options: The View tab of Explorer View — Folder contains a large number of option boxes. At the top of this panel you can opt to make all of your folders look like the current folder, or to reset all to their original style. The *Advanced Settings* contain the option boxes marked:

Remember each folder's new setting
Display the full path on title bar
Hide file extensions for known file types
Show Map Network Drive button on toolbar
Show file attributes in Detail View
Show pop-up description for folder and desktop items
Allow all-uppercase names

The *Hidden files* buttons are:

Do not show hidden or system files
Do not show hidden files
Show all files

The *Visual Settings* are:

Hide icons when desktop is viewed as a Web page
Smooth edges of screen fonts
Show window contents while dragging

Start menu: see entry for Start menu

Favourites: see entry for Favourites

Toolbars: In addition to the ready-made toolbars, you can create a toolbar from the contents of any folder. For example, you could create a toolbar for the Recycle Bin, or a toolbar that displays icons for each of your documents.

To create a toolbar for a folder, right-click any blank space in the taskbar and in the *Toolbars* set click *New Toolbar*. Select the folder you want to use, which might contain documents and/or shortcuts, and click. The toolbar will appear on the Taskbar, allowing access to the folder and its contents. You can drag the toolbar to the Desktop, or use the *Toolbars* set to clear the tick against the name of this toolbar and so remove it.

Fonts

General: A font is a design for printed characters. Font designs can be serif or sans-serif. A serif font uses a more elaborate design, with small 'hooks' at the ends of letters. The sans-serif fonts use plain designs in which it can be difficult to distinguish the letter 'ell' from the numeric 'one'. Serif fonts are used for long text items, because a serif font is more readable. Sans-serif fonts are used to break up the monotony of long text, particularly for captions and quotes, and also for short documents. Windows 98 keeps fonts in a folder of their own, and has several font-management facilities so that you can use your fonts in all of your Windows programs. Large collections of fonts, typically 1500 or more, are available on CD-ROM.

Using fonts: By default, the text that you see in Windows (such as menu names and lists) uses a sans-serif font. You can change this by using the Control Panel, either from Explorer or from Start — Settings — Control Panel. Click *Display*, and use the *Appearance* tab. The Item panel contains a list of the essential parts of a window, several of which (such as title bar, icon, menu, etc.) use fonts. For each item that uses a font, you can click the arrowhead on the *Font* space to see the list of fonts available to you. You can then change the font and the size (see **Notes**, below).

You may not like the effect of your changes unless you remember that small sizes of serif fonts do not look clear on a 640 × 480 screen, and that a change of colour of font or background can often make a font look clearer. Printed work always looks better than its appearance on the screen might suggest.

TrueType fonts: Your programs that make use of fonts will be able to select from the set of fonts that you install with Windows 98 and any fonts that you subsequently add. You should use fonts from the TrueType set for any document that will be printed, because the printout of such fonts matches their screen appearance – this cannot be guaranteed for the ordinary screen fonts that are not marked with the T_T logo.

Adding/Removing: Fonts can be added or removed using the Control Panel. Click on the *Fonts* icon and wait until the *Fonts* menu appears. To add a font, you will need a floppy or CD-ROM that contains fonts. Click on File — Install New Font. You will see the *Fonts* installation panel appear, with a list of fonts (blank), and boxes for *Folder* and *Drive*. You will need to change the drive and folder entries to match the source of your new fonts (floppy or CD-ROM), and when you do this the names of the new fonts will appear in the fonts list. You can select one or more fonts. If you want to install all of the fonts from a set, click on the *Select All* button. Make sure that the box marked *Copy fonts to Fonts folder* is ticked, and then click on the *OK* button.

To delete a font, use the *Font Manager* as above and select the name of the font you want to delete. Click the *Delete* key or use File — Delete. You will not be able to select a font if you have opted to *Hide Font Variations* (see Font management, following).

Font Management: The *Font Manager* of Control Panel allows you to use some actions that are not available from other menus. The File menu contains *Open, Print, Install New Font, Create Shortcut, Delete, Rename* and *Properties*. Of these, *Open* and *Print* are used to show the appearance of fonts on a sample page, and cannot be used unless the file MFC30.DLL is present in the WINDOWS\SYSTEM folder. The *Install* option has been dealt with, above, and the other actions on selected font files correspond to the Explorer actions of the same name.

Windows 98 assistant

The *Edit* menu also corresponds to that of Explorer, but there are some items in the View menu that are unique to Font Manager. *List Fonts by Similarity* allows you to pick one font in the heading of a list, and show the other fonts graded *as Very Similar, Fairly Similar, Not Similar* or *No PANOSE Information Available*. This type of listing is useful if you are trying to match fonts. The *Hide Variations* option can be selected so that each font is shown as a single entry, ignoring style variations such as Normal, Bold, Italic, and so on. This makes the fonts list look rather less daunting.

The *Options* set of View contains a panel with four tabs. Click the *Folder* tab to see two options for viewing multiple folders. You can use a separate window for each folder (the default) or use a window whose contents change for each folder – this latter option makes it much easier to close down the folder window. The *View* tab and *File Types* tab correspond to the same displays in Explorer, and the *TrueType* tab allows you to show only the TrueType fonts in the Font Manager display.

Help fonts: Click Help and click a topic. On the Help window click Options — Font. Select *Small, Medium* or *Large*.

Internet fonts: Click View — Fonts and select the size from the range *Largest, Larger, Medium, Smaller,* and *Smallest*.

Notes: Font size is measured in terms of point, with one point equal to $^{1}/_{72}$". The size is the **height** of any capital letter (because lower-case letters are not all of the same height), and because of the differing designs of fonts, you can find that a sentence typed using several different fonts of the same point size will take up surprisingly different amounts of space, because of the different width of letters in different fonts but of the same point size.

If you install additional programs that make use of fonts you may find that your hard drive becomes overloaded with font files. You should check at intervals how many fonts you really need and use and remove the others. Back them up or make a note of their origin if you feel that you might use some of them subsequently.

Note: If you need to use the Euro currency symbol, a font can be downloaded from the site: http:// www.xs4all.nl. This symbol will not appear correctly on a computer that does not have the font unless you use an option (as in Word, for example) to embed the font into your document.

Go menu

General: The Go menu appears in both forms of Explorer and is concerned with moving between Web pages or folders, and contains several items designed to make this easy.

Back: Will move to the previous page or item. Shortcut is Alt-← or the toolbar left-arrow icon.

Forward: Will move to the next page or item. Shortcut is Alt-→ or the toolbar right-arrow icon.

Up one level: Will move back one layer of folders when you are exploring folders and files.

Note that the Forward and Back icons on the toolbar have small arrowheads that can be clicked to show the range of sites that can be accessed in this way.

Home page: Displays the Home (Start) page, for which the default is http://home.microsoft.com/. You can change to a more convenient start page (from a UK source) by displaying your preferred start page and using View — Internet Options — Home page and clicking the *Use*

Current button when *Start page* is selected in the page list that appears. A blank page can be selected for faster starting, or you can click the *Use Default* button. If most of your use of the Internet is in searching, you can make the *Home Page* a search engine page by using the *Use Current* button when you are about to launch a search.

Channel Guide: Will open the Channel Guide Web page.

Search the Web: Displays the search page, for which the default is the Microsoft search page.

Mail: Switches to the Outlook Express mail program so that you can send an e-mail message or read an incoming e-mail message.

News: Switches to the Outlook Express news program so that you can read information from a newsgroup or make your own contributions.

My Computer: You can move to this overall view of your computer, showing the hardware items such as printer and drives, as well as Control Panel and Dial-up Networking.

Address Book: Click this item to get to your name and address list, which can also contain e-mail addresses and telephone numbers and other data.

Graphics, Internet

General: Text can be downloaded much faster than graphics, but some graphics content is useful for many types of Internet pages. You may need to balance your need to see pictures with the time you can spare for downloading images. Note that pictures are **not** saved when you save a page to a file. Many Internet pictures are transmitted in a coded format called JPEG, using the JPG or JPE extension letters.

Displaying or hiding: Click View — Internet Options — Advanced and click the *Show pictures* box in the *Multimedia* section to enable or disable pictures. Even if *Show pictures* is disabled, you can still view an image by clicking on the icon with the **right-hand** mouse button and then clicking on *Show Picture*.

Saving as file: You can save an image from a page by clicking on the picture icon using the **right-hand** mouse button, and then click the *Save Target As* menu item. You will need to supply a filename. Note that this must be done while you are online because the picture information must be downloaded.

Desktop wallpaper: You can use any graphics image downloaded over the net as graphics wallpaper for Windows. Display the page that contains the image, click with the **right-hand** mouse button on the image, and on the menu that appears click the *Set as Wallpaper* item.

Hardware

General: When Windows 98 is installed, it keeps a record of all the hardware (drives, monitor, modem, printer, etc.) that exists at that time. If you subsequently change your hardware you need to do so in a way that ensures that these records (see the entry for **registry**) are correctly maintained. This must be done after the mechanical work of bolting in and connecting a new piece of hardware has been satisfactorily completed. You can, however, remove hardware from the records without physically removing the equipment (this will disable the hardware).

Adding hardware: Use Control Panel from Explorer or from Start — Settings — Control Panel. Click on *Add New Hardware*. This starts the title panel of a Wizard, and you need to click the *Next* button. The next panel asks if you want to have Windows automatically detect your new hardware. This is the advised option, because if Windows detects the hardware it will almost certainly ensure that the correct software driver is installed. If you opt for manual detection then you will probably need a disc containing drivers from the supplier of the new hardware.

The type of hardware that can be detected is listed as:

1394 Bus controller	3D accelerators	CD-ROM controller
CXP	Display Adapters	Floppy disc controllers
Global positioning devices	Hard drive controllers	Human interface device
Imaging device	Infrared devices	Keyboard
Memory Technology Driver (MTD)	Modem	Modem Voice
Mouse	Multi-function adapters	Network adapters
Other devices	PCMCIA socket	Port (LPT or COM)
Printer	SCSI controller	Sound, Video, Games controller
System Devices	Tape drive controllers	Universal serial bus controller

Before you start to use the auto-detect action, shut down all programs other than Explorer. When you start the auto-detect action, the progress is indicated by a bar-graph display, and the action may take several minutes. Do not worry if there is no change in the indicator for a minute or so, as long as you can hear your hard drive working. When the action is completed you will see a report on the new hardware that Windows has detected and on the driver that has been used.

If Windows does not detect a new hardware item, or if you opt for manual detection, you will see a list of manufacturers and equipment from which you can select. Click the *Have Disk* button to install a driver that has been supplied by a manufacturer, and be guided by the Wizard.

Hardware conflicts: If a new item of hardware refuses to operate correctly this may be due to conflicts, usually when older hardware is in use. Windows 98 can help to resolve such conflicts by using a Wizard called the *Hardware Conflict Troubleshooter*. Click this item in the *Help* index and then click on the box labelled *Click here to start the hardware conflict troubleshooter*. Follow the instructions that appear in each step until the problem is resolved.

Hardware profiles: These are files that are used to allow Windows to adapt to different configurations and which apply mainly to portable machines whose hardware connections depend on whether the machine is docked or free. This is a specialised topic which needs experience, and will not be covered in this book.

Note: You do not need to use *Add Hardware* if you add another hard drive to your system, only if you change the hard drive controller. See also the entry for **Plug and Play**.

Help

General: On-screen help is available on many topics, but the information can often be patchy, and sometimes you find that you are switching between panels without getting any useful advice. Sometimes selecting a Help item will provide the information on a previous item. Some of the most useful help is the **context-sensitive** type (see entry), and where this is not indicated by a question-mark icon, it may be found as a *What's This* item in the Help menu.

Starting help: Click the *Help* menu on the header bar, or press the F1 key. You will see the *Help* menu for Windows

Windows 98 assistant

98 if no other program is active. If you fetch the wrong *Help* set (from Word, for example), minimise all programs so that you see the Desktop of Windows 98. The other route to Windows 98 Help (which provides Windows 98 Help even if other programs are running) is Start — Help.

Help Topics: When the main Help window appears, it is divided into *Contents*, *Index* and *Find*. The *Contents* section is aimed at the newcomer to Windows, and the initial window shows the topics *of Introducing Internet Explorer 4.??*, *Introducing Windows*, *How To...*, *Tips and Tricks*, *Troubleshooting*, and *Virtual Private Networking*. Click on an item represented by the book icon to expand it, and double-click on other (book icon) items that appear in an expanded list to find the advice.

The more experienced user will normally use the *Index* section. In the header of this window, you can delete any default text with the *Delete* key and start to type the words you are looking for. As you type, corresponding *Help* items will be selected, and you can click on the *Display* button to show the *Help* notes associated with that item. Cross-referencing is used, so that the same topic can be reached by typing different words. For example, you can find the same Help item by typing *fixing errors in discs* or by typing *discs, repairing*.

The *Find* tab starts a form of database which scans the *Help* files for words that you type. This is not exactly foolproof – you will get advice on fixing disc errors, for example if you type *fix*, but not when you have completed typing *fixing*. The *Options* button can be used to determine how you want to make use of the letters that you have typed. The first section is headed *Search for Topics Containing* and the default option is *All the words you typed in any order*. The other options are *At least one of the words you typed* and *The words you typed in exact order*. There is a check box labelled *Display matching phrases* which will show in the display the words that follow the phrase that you typed. This makes the search slower but helps to locate what you want.

The *Show Words that* section contains as its default *begin with the characters you typed*, but you can click the arrowhead to use the options of *contain the characters you typed*, *end with the character you typed* and *match the characters you typed*. In the *Begin Search* section you can opt for *After you Click the Find Now Button* or *Immediately After a Keystroke*. The checkbox in this section is labelled *Wait for a Pause Before Searching* and applies only if you opt for searching immediately after a keystroke.

The buttons of the *Options* panel are *OK*, *Cancel* and *Files*. Click the *Files* button to narrow the search down to one or more of the *Specialised Help files* (which are all selected by default, with a *Select All* button to use if you have selected a single file and want to search all).

Help on top: *On Top* means that a *Help* window will always appear over any other window, so that the *Help* text is never covered unless you drag the *Help* window out of sight. With a *Help* topic window displayed, click on *Options*. Click the *Help on Top* item, and then click *On Top* so that this option is ticked. If you click *Default*, some *Help* windows will be on top and others not. You can click *Not on Top* if you want *Help* windows to be covered by other windows that are opened later.

Help options: The *Options* button of a *Help* window contains the *Help on Top* item as noted above, and several other useful items. The *Annotate* option (if present) allows you to make notes about a *Help* item that can be displayed when that item is called up. When you use this option by clicking *Annotation*, you will see a panel appear into which you can type your note. The buttons beside the panel are labelled *Save*, *Cancel*, *Delete*, *Copy* and *Paste*. Use the *Save* button

Windows 98 assistant

when you have completed your note, or use *Cancel* if you have second thoughts. *Delete* is used when you want to erase an existing note. *Copy* is used to copy selected text in the *Annotation*, and *Paste* can be used if you have copied other text to the Clipboard and want to paste it into the *Annotation* space. When an annotation exists in a *Help* panel, a paper-clip symbol appears next to the title of the *Help* panel. Click on this symbol to display the annotation.

The *Copy* option is used to copy selected *Help* text to the Clipboard. Once this has been done, you can paste the text into another program such as Notepad or Word. The *Print Topic* option will print the whole of a *Help* panel (the printer must be switched on and on line). A new page will be taken for each topic. The *Font* options allows you to specify *Small*, *Normal* or *Large* font size for the text in the *Help* panel. Finally, the *Use System Colors* option can be clicked so that the colours used in *Help* match the colour scheme you are using for other items. When you alter this *Colors* option, you will have to close the *Help* file and restart it to see the effect.

Web Help: Click this heading to get support online from Microsoft. This delivers a message and contains a link called Support Online. Clicking on this link will make contact through your modem with a Microsoft site that you can use to search for help.

Notes: The *Back* button in a *Help* panel can be used to return to the last *Help* panel you opened (not to the index). Return to the index by clicking on the *Help Topics* button.

Some topics that appeared in the Help for Windows 95 do not appear in Windows 98, though you may see references to them in error messages.

You can make a quick copy of text in a Help file by selecting the text, right-clicking and clicking Copy. You can then paste the text into another application.

History

General: The History folder contains a list, the *History list*, of links to all the pages you have viewed using Internet Explorer, not just pages viewed in the current session. If you cannot find a page that you have previously viewed by using the *Go* menu, open the *History* folder. The *History list* is maintained for a period that by default is likely to be 20 to 30 days, but you can alter this setting. You can see the History List in Windows Explorer by using View — Explorer Bar — History.

Opening: Click the History button in the Toolbar, or use View — Explorer Bar — History. You will see a display of date ranges starting on a Monday (such as Week of May 4) and also for the last few days. Click the range that you want to view and view the contents. If you are offline and you click an item that needs to be downloaded again you will be reminded and given the option to stay offline or to download.

Maintaining list: Click View — Internet Options — General and look at the *History* section. You can alter the *Days* setting to suit your use of this action. You can specify up to 999 days, but remember that a large number here might require an inordinate amount of disc space to be used. You can clear the list by using the *Clear History* button. This does not necessarily clear the files that the History List pointed to.

Note: If you are working offline and have specified a short life for temporary files, you will see the pointer change to a diagonal bar shape over older items in the History list. This means that these items can no longer be taken from the hard drive since they have been erased. You can. however, download them again by going online.

HTML

General: HTML is an abbreviation of Hypertext markup language, and is a form of programming language used to create Web pages and to insert links into your text documents.

Since this is a specialised subject that requires some programming experience, it is not covered further here, but Windows 98 contains a Web authoring package in the form of Front Page Express.

Hyperlinks

General: A hyperlink can appear in either version of Explorer or in a document as a word or phrase in colour and (usually) underlined, or an icon (plain picture or 3D image), and is used to follow up a reference by looking at another page of information, a picture, a video, or hearing a sound. When the mouse pointer is placed over a hyperlink, the pointer shape will change to a hand. Clicking on a hyperlink while you are online will download another file for a document, picture, video or sound.

Links toolbar: The *Links* toolbar contains a set of hyperlink icons to Web sites on which information is updated frequently. Click any link while online to download the appropriate page.

Cancelling: If a hyperlink takes too long to download, click the *Stop* icon (X) on the toolbar.

Dragging: A hyperlink can be dragged to the desktop, or to any other visible location, to provide a shortcut (you must be online to make use of a shortcut of this type).

Options: You can enable or disable underlining of hyperlinks, or alter the colour for links, by using View — Internet Options — General.

HyperTerminal

General: HyperTerminal is a communications program that would take a complete book in its own right to explain thoroughly. What follows is simply a brief outline of its capabilities. You computer must be fitted with a modem, correctly installed, to make use of HyperTerminal. You may not need to use HyperTerminal – for example, if you want access to the Internet or to e-mail, there are specialised programs that are much more suitable. You can use HyperTerminal for making access to bulletin boards or to other computer services that are accessible on telephone numbers that you know.

Starting HyperTerminal: Click on Start — Programs — Accessories — Communications — HyperTerminal. This does **not** launch HyperTerminal right away but displays a set of files of which one is **Hypertrm.exe**, the terminal program. When you click on this file the terminal program will start. You could make a shortcut direct to Hypertrm if you are likely to make use of the program frequently.

Note that if you want to switch between HyperTerminal and other programs you should click on the HyperTerminal window or use the Alt-Tab method, because clicking on the HyperTerminal icon in the Taskbar will bring you back to the folder which contains the Hypertrm program. On your first use of HyperTerminal you will be asked if you want to update, and you can type a name and select an icon for a new connection (to a bulletin board or some form of information provider such as AT&T or MCI.

You will need to create a name for each different contact, and in the example that follows we'll look at how to connect to a bulletin board in the UK. You will be asked for a filename, and the name of the bulletin board is appropriate here.

You will then see the next form which requires the country code, area code and telephone number — the default that appears is your own number if you already have a modem fitted and use Dial-Up Networking. The *Connect using* space will show the name of modem you use. In this form, you can fill in the number for the bulletin board. You can opt not to use Country and area codes if you are using a local number.

You will now see a *Connect* panel, showing the number that you want to dial. Your location is shown as *Default location*. The *Modify* button allows you to alter the phone number if you want to, and also provides for altering some terminal actions by way of a *Dialing Properties* panel. These settings should be left at their defaults unless you are experienced with communications and you know what alterations to make. Click the *Dial* button to make the connection.

From then on, how you proceed depends on how you want to use the facilities of the bulletin board, which has nothing to do with HyperTerminal. The screen will show you what keys have to be pressed to obtain various facilities, and you can type messages to the Sysop (bulletin board system operator), look at files, download software and so on.

Disconnect: Click on the disconnect icon to stop the action if, for example, you have connected at an expensive time or if you simply wanted to check that your settings were correct. When you know that settings are correct you should use the *Save* item on the *File* menu of HyperTerminal to save your session file so that you can make use of it again without the need to enter numbers and options. This ensures that you need set up for a particular contact once only.

Sending a file: When you click on the Transfer — Send File option, you will see a form appear which asks you for a filename and you can also select your protocol type with the default of *Zmodem* (seven other popular options are available). You can fill in the name with a filename that you know (with path), or you can use the *Browse* button to locate and select a file. When the *Send* button becomes active you can click it to send your file to the remote computer.

Receiving a file: The Transfer — Receive file option also provides for a choice of protocols, and you can select a folder to receive the file. The default here is the *HyperTerminal* folder, but you can set up a folder for each particular connection if you want. The default protocol for receiving is *Zmodem with Crash Recovery*.

When you send data you should always prepare it as a file before you use HyperTerminal. Remember that the telephone charges are ticking away all the time you are on line, so typing more than a few words while you are connected can be a costly business.

- You can also opt to deal with the capture and sending of text files, using simpler and faster protocols.

Note: Windows 98 regards HyperTerminal as a program for communicating with computers that are **not** running Windows, such as for links with bulletin boards that might use different types of computers. If you are communicating with a computer that is running Windows 98 you are advised to use the Dial-Up Networking action rather than

Windows 98 assistant

HyperTerminal. This is a matter of taste — you might not want to use the complications of Dial-Up Networking or you might not have space for the extra files that it uses. HyperTerminal can communicate with any computer that is connected online, whether it runs Windows or not, and you need Dial-up Networking only if you want the ability to work as if you were networked to the other computer.

Icons

General: Each file, as seen in Explorer, carries an icon. In some cases, particularly for older MS-DOS programs, the icons for different programs are identical, but icons for Windows programs are usually distinctive. Icons for MS-DOS program files can be changed if required, but this action is not necessarily available for document files (unless you use a different method), nor for most Windows programs unless the manufacturer has provided for a choice. You **can**, however, always change the icon that is used for a shortcut.

The use of icons is extended in Windows 98 by the *Web page* form of display.

Taskbar icons: The four icons that Windows 98 places into the Taskbar are intended for Internet working, and can be clicked to start Internet Explorer, Outlook Express, the Desktop, and Channels.

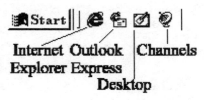

Icon Size: You can alter the size of icons used in an Explorer display. With Explorer running, select *View* and then *Large Icons* or *Small Icons*. This does not permit you to alter the size of a single selected icon. You can also opt for *List* or *Details* for non-icon displays.

You can also change the icon sizes that are used in the Start menu. Click Start — Settings — Taskbar and look for the checkbox marked *Show Small Icons in Start Menu*. Tick this box for small icons, and leave it unticked for larger icons.

Change program/shortcut Icon: With an MS-DOS program file, or a shortcut, selected in the Explorer display, click on File — Properties — Program — Change Icon. You will see a set of (typically 38) icons in a display that can be scrolled sideways. For some Windows programs, the set of available icons may be limited or there will be no *Change Icon* button in the *Properties* panel. Typically you will find a very limited choice for shortcuts, and no *Change Icon* button for most Windows programs. You can use the *Browse* button if it is present to find a larger range of icons, notably in the C:\WINDOWS folder, where you can browse the MORICONS.DLL file. Set the *Browse* action *Files of Type* box to *Libraries* so that you can find the DLL files more easily. Another set of icons is contained in WINDOWS\SYSTEM\SHELL32.DLL) folder, and there are also icons on the Windows 98 CD.

Change document icon: On the Explorer display, click View — Options and click on the *File Types* tab. The display shows the registered document file types with icons and extension letters. Click on a file type, and then on the *Edit* button. You will now see a *Change Icon* button, and you can change to any other icon that is displayed, or browse for one of the libraries that contains more icons.

Desktop Icons: Open Control Panel either from Explorer or from Start — Settings. Click on *Display*, and select the

Windows 98 assistant

Appearance tab. Open out the *Item* display so that you can see the entries *Icon*, *Icon Spacing (Horizontal)* and *Icon Spacing (Vertical)*. These settings can be changed to alter the size and spacing of the Desktop icons – they have no effect on other icons.

Notes: The default icons should be used unless you find that two programs are using very similar icons.

Icons, Internet Explorer

General: The picture shows the standard set of icons on the Toolbar of Internet Explorer. These are usually labelled, but the label name can be turned off using View — Options — General — Toolbar and clicking on *Text labels*. The illustration shows the icons in two separate lines.

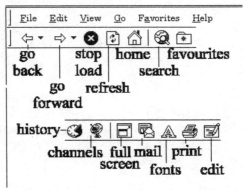

Icons, Mail

General: The picture shows the standard set of icons on the Toolbar of Outlook Express, used for Email. The icons display can be turned on or off using View — Toolbar. There is no option for turning off the labels next to the icons

Icons, News

General: The picture shows the standard set of icons on the Toolbar of Outlook Express used for News. The icons display can be turned on or off using View — Toolbar. There is no option for turning off the labels next to the icons

Improving performance, Web

General: Even if you are using a modem which is as fast as can be obtained, the time needed to download some types of data is excessive, particularly at busy times. You can greatly speed up performance by opting not to download time-consuming large files of pictures, sounds or video.

Options: Click View — Options — General, and in the *Multimedia* section clear one or more of the boxes. These are labelled *Show Pictures*, *Play Sounds* and *Play Videos*.

Windows 98 assistant

Picture override: If you have opted not to download picture files, you can override this global command by clicking with the right-hand mouse button on the hyperlink for the picture, and selecting the *Show Picture* menu item. If a picture is still visible after clearing the *Show Pictures* box, click View — Refresh to remove the picture.

Installing W'98 components

General: Windows 95 installation allowed users to opt for a 'typical' installation or possibly a minimal installation rather than the full installation of all possible components. Windows 98 dispenses with such options, because the task of removing unwanted programs and installing others is easier than it was for Windows 95.

Altering Setup: Close all running programs other than Explorer. Start Control Panel from Explorer or from Start — Settings. Click on *Add/Remove Programs*, and when the panel appears, click on the tab marked *Windows Setup*. You will see a list of Windows components arranged in groups. Click on a group and then on the *Details* button to see the list of individual programs in the group. You can opt to select the whole group (black tick against the group name) or individual programs (black tick against selected programs, black tick on greyed background against the group). Click the *OK* button to get from a *Detail* display to the overall display, and click the *OK* button on the main display to start installation, which will require the Windows 98 CD-ROM or the floppy set to be inserted.

You can also remove components in this way, clicking to remove the tick from programs or groups that were originally ticked. This is preferable to deleting the files using Explorer because you may be able to identify the main EXE files of a program but you cannot be sure that you can find the DLL and other associated files.

Notes: Do **not** delete any DLL file in an Explorer display unless you are absolutely certain that it is redundant, because many DLL files are shared by more than one program.

You can also use the **Disk Cleanup** action for removing unwanted Windows components or other programs. See the separate entry for this heading.

Internet Explorer

General: Though Internet Explorer is incorporated into Windows 98, you will still have to find an information provider (IP). The cost of the IP service varies greatly, and this aspect is covered in the entry for **access, Internet**. This current entry covers the features of Internet Explorer in Windows 98.

Addresses: A Web address typically starts http://www, and if you omit the http:// part it will be automatically inserted. You can tick the *Use AutoComplete* option (in View — Internet Options — Advanced) if you want more of a name to be completed automatically for you. If you type part of a name and press Ctrl–Enter the name will be completed, and if a name can be completed as you type it this will be done. These actions do not always provide a correct name, however, and the action can sometimes be annoyingly obstructive, so that the option is often better left unticked.

An Internet address (sometimes called a **URL**, or Uniform Resource Locator) typically starts with a protocol name, followed by the name of the organization that maintains the site; the suffix identifies the kind of organization it is. (A protocol is a set of rules and standards that enable computers to exchange information.)

For example, the address http://www.yale.edu/ provides the following information.

http:	This Web server uses the http: protocol.
www	This site is on the World Wide Web.
yale	The Web server is at Yale University.
.edu	This is an educational institution.

Generally, commercial site addresses end with .com, and government site addresses end with .gov.

If the address points to a specific page, additional information — such as a port name, the directory in which the page is located, and the name of the page file — is included. Web pages authored by using HTML (Hypertext Markup Language) often end with an .htm or .html extension.

When you are viewing a Web page, the page's address appears in the Address bar in the browser. This should have been enabled using View — Toolbars.

Channels: see separate entry for Channels.

Universal Explorer: You can transform Internet Explorer into a universal version that can do all that is available in both versions. This hinges on the Go — My Computer option. Clicking on this will provide the My Computer view, and if this has been changed (see the **My Computer** entry) to an Explorer view you can click the C:\ entry to obtain a set of folders and files that you would see in Windows Explorer. Furthermore, when you use Go — Home Page or any other return to Web browsing, Explorer will still contain the Tools item from Windows Explorer. In Web mode, you can use View — Internet Options and in My Computer mode you can use the View — Folder options. If this format of Explorer is active when you switch off, it will reappear when you restart the computer. If you have closed Explorer, you can regain your settings by running Internet Explorer and using the Go — My Computer option again.

Keyboard

General: The keyboard that is connected to your computer will normally be the one intended for UK use, but some bargain-offer computers come with a US keyboard which will have no £ sign, and with the positions of some characters, notably inverted commas, altered. You can opt to use any language with your standard keyboard, and other types of keyboards, including the Microsoft Natural Keyboard, are available. If you want to plug in and use a different keyboard, see the entry for **hardware.** A wide range of options can be used to alter the behaviour of your keyboard without altering the hardware itself.

Change key actions: Start Control Panel either from Explorer or from Start — Settings. Click on *Keyboard* to see the 3-tab panel. The first tab is labelled *Speed*, and concerns the repeat action. You can alter the delay period between pressing down a key and starting the repeat action, and you can alter the rate at which a character repeats once the repeat action starts. If you have been used to a manual non-electric typewriter you might want to opt for a long delay and a slow repetition rate, because you may have acquired the bad habit of pausing with a key held down. If you are accustomed to a computer keyboard, you are more likely to want to use a short delay and a fast repetition rate.

- You can also change the cursor blink speed in this panel. Choose a rate which is fast enough for you to see that the cursor **is** blinking, but not so fast that it becomes hypnotic.

The second tab is labelled *Language* and it allows you to select the language that you want to use from your keyboard. There is a wide choice of languages available when you click the *Add* button, and you can select one or more to be made available. If you want another language to be the default, you can click the *Set as Default* button. You can also use the option buttons at the bottom of the panel to set a method of changing language, either with Left-Alt and Shift, Ctrl and Shift, or without any key method of changing language. Tick the box to make the language setting appear on the Windows 98 Taskbar. For a selected language, you can click the *Properties* button to see what type of keyboard is normally used for that language. The keyboard set that can be accommodated ranges from Afrikaans to Ukranian, much the same as the *Language* selection list.

- You can also change the driver file for your keyboard by starting Control Panel and clicking on *System*, followed by *Device Manager*, *Keyboard*, and the keyboard type you are using.

Modifying action: The keyboard action can be modified, particularly by using the Accessibility options of Windows 98 (to add these options, see the entry for **Installing W98 components**). See the entry for **Accessibility** for details.

Notes: If you set your keyboard for another language and switch to that language you will not be able to use tools such as the spellcheck action of Word unless you have installed a dictionary file for that language.

- If your physical (hardware) keyboard is not suited to the language you will have problems with characters that are specific to that language. Use the Character Map to insert characters that do not appear on your keyboard.

Laptop computer

Windows 98 supports the use of laptop computers by way of the facilities of Power management, Briefcase, Direct Computer Connection, Deferred printing and Docking detection.

Power management: Installing a laptop computer will place additional icons into Windows. In particular, Control Panel contains a *Power Management* item that allows you to control the shutdown of the hard drive and the display when the machine is idle. The item listed as *Allow Windows to Manage power use on this computer* must be checked. Note that a desktop computer also will allow for shutting down the hard drive. You should also opt for *Show Battery Meter On The Taskbar*. This icon can then be clicked to show the remaining expected battery life before recharging.

Briefcase: See the separate Briefcase heading.

Direct computer connection: see the separate item with this heading.

Deferred printing: You can use a print command on your laptop computer even if you do not have a printer connected. You must have installed the correct version of Windows 98 for laptops, and have turned on printer spooling. Before you print, click the icon for the printer you will use and then click File — Work Offline. Do not confuse this with the *Work Offline* relating to the Web.

All documents you 'print' will be stored until you click the Work Offline command again. If you use your laptop with a docking station, documents you have stored will be printed when you start Windows in the docking mode.

Docking detection: Windows 98 can detect whether your laptop is docked or undocked, and will use the correct settings if you have specified differences.

135

Links bar

General: The *Links* toolbar of either version of Explorer carries a set of icons (hyperlinks) which open Web pages on which information is often updated. The toolbar can be hidden when not in use — it may appear at the right hand side of the Address toolbar in Windows Explorer.

Open/close toolbar: Click View — Toolbars — Links to enable or disable the *Links* toolbar.

Appearance: You can change the appearance of the sections of the toolbar by dragging or collapsing, though you cannot drag any toolbar outside the normal toolbar area (unlike the taskbar of Windows 98). You can click on the words *Address* or *Links* to drag that portion of toolbar upwards, resulting in a toolbar which shows the main icons with *Address* and *Links* as buttons. You can also drag the thick lower border of the main toolbar so that the labels disappear, leaving only (smaller) icons. On a single collapsed toolbar, thick boundary lines can also be dragged sideways to reveal other toolbar portions such as *Address* or *Links*. These changes can be used to provide more space for the page to be viewed.

Maintenance wizard

The maintenance wizard is designed to assist you in keeping your computer performing at its best by scheduling the use of Defragmenter, ScanDisk and other utilities. The snag is that if the computer is not running when the scheduled action is due, the action cannot be carried out. Maintenance wizard is therefore more suited to computers that are kept running through the night, or for extended daytime use.

Start wizard: From the Start button, use Programs — Accessories — System Tools — Maintenance Wizard. You will see a panel that has the default of *Perform maintenance now*, with the option of *Change my maintenance settings of schedule*. If you do the maintenance at once, the actions will be performed in sequence, deleting unwanted files, checking the hard drive for errors and speeding up your most frequently used programs by rearranging their position on the hard drive.

Settings: If you use the Settings option, you have the choice of *Express maintenance*, using the most common settings, or *Custom*, allowing you to select settings. Using *Express* gives a choice of times as *Night* (Midnight to 3:00 AM), *Days* (Noon to 3:00 PM) or *Evenings* (8:00 PM to 11:00 PM). When you select a time range and click on the *Next* button, you can finish the Wizard, with an option to perform each task for the first time when you click the *Finish* button.

If you opt for *Custom* you have the same choice of *Nights*, *Days* or *Evenings* along with a *Custom* setting that allows the current setting to be used once you have set times. Pressing the *Next* button leads to a schedule pane in which you can opt to defragment regularly or to turn off defragmenting. In the pane that shows a defragmentation schedule time you can click the *Reschedule* button to alter the time, or click *Settings* if you want to alter the default drive.

The *Next* button then leads to a similar set of choices for using ScanDisk, and following this you can schedule the deletion of unwanted files. The *Custom* settings also end with the option to perform all of the tasks at the time when you click the *Finish* button.

Media devices

General: Media Player is used along with coded sound or video data, and is useful if you intend to make use of multimedia. Your computer should contain a sound card, correctly installed. For animated video using larger window sizes, you may need a specialised video card, but in general you cannot expect the standard of video replay that you can obtain from a TV receiver and video recorder. The sound files for Media Player are held in the Windows\Media folder. You do **not** need to use Media Player separately if you are using a multi-media program such as Encarta from a CD-ROM.

Media Player files: Click Start — Programs — Accessories — Multimedia — Media Player. If your sound card is Soundblaster this will appear between Multimedia and Media Player. If you frequently want to use Media Player, make a shortcut to it in the Start menu. You can place the shortcut in the *Startup* folder if you want to use Media Player each time you start Windows 98. When the panel appears, click *Device*, which will list, typically, *Video for Windows*, *Sound, MIDI sequencer*, and *CD Audio*. Data files, such as WAV files, are held in the C:\Windows\Media folder.

Starting play: With an appropriate device selected and a file loaded, use the Media Player controls which are illustrated here for a music CD. The pointer has been placed on the CD track to be played, and the *Play* symbol clicked. The illustration shows the actions corresponding to the symbols, which are the standard symbols used on video recorders.

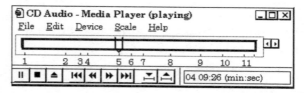

The less-familiar symbols are for moving to a selection mark (earlier or later in the file) and for creating these start and stop selection marks. These features are used if you want to be able to go to a portion of the file quickly and in particular if you want to repeat a portion of a file.

- You can simplify the Player display, which is particularly useful for CD play. Click on the title bar so that the display changes to one of tracks only, with a *Play* and a *Stop* symbol. You can click on the title bar again to restore the original panel.

- Remember that if your only use of Media Player is to play audio CDs, you should use CD Player instead, and set it up so that playing is automatically started when the CD is inserted, see the entry for **CD Player**.

Options: The Edit — Options menu content varies according to what type of multimedia object is being edited. For an Audio CD, for example, you can opt for *Auto Rewind* and *Auto Repeat*. The *OLE Object* section is used for all suitable objects, and there are selection boxes (taking the Audio CD object again as an example) for *Control bar on Playback*, *Play in Client Document*, and *Dither the Picture to VGA Colours* (this last choice is greyed out for an audio CD).

Notes: In general, it is better to reserve Media Player for items other than Audio CD.

See also CD Player, Multimedia

Memory

General: Memory, both the amount and the way in which it is used, is very important to the running of Windows 98. If you have insufficient memory then many actions, particularly when you are running large programs like Word-97 or switching between several programs, will be very slow. Windows 98 needs **at least** 16 Mbyte. Speed is very noticeably improved when you upgrade to 32 Mbyte, and there is another improvement, not so great, when you upgrade from 32 Mbyte to 64 Mbyte. If your computer is a Pentium type using SIMM EDO memory, you must upgrade with SIMM memory strips installed in matching pairs, but if DIMM memory is used you can upgrade in single units. Some computers will not accept a mixture of memory types, others allow DIMMs to be inserted in sockets that do not conflict with SIMM boards.

Installing memory: Memory is installed by inserting SIMM units, usually of 8 Mbyte or more each, into the memory slots. The usual method is to slide the SIMM into its holder with the memory unit held at an angle, and then rotate the whole set until the SIMM clicks into place. There are books devoted to upgrading which illustrate the method in detail. No other action is needed — after the memory has been clipped into place, the computer will recognise the memory when it is switched on, and Windows 98 will make use of it.

If your computer can use the DIMM type of memory (these can be installed singly) you will need to check if SIMMs have to be removed to allow the use of DIMM. It is likely that in the future SIMM types will be discontinued.

Optimising use: It is possible to have adequate memory but make inefficient use of it. Open Control Panel from Explorer or from Start — Settings and click *System*. Click the *Performance* tab of the panel, and then click the *Virtual Memory* tab. You will see that the default option is in use, marked as *Let Windows manage my virtual memory settings (recommended)*. This is good advice, but if you have adequate hard drive space you can often achieve better performance by using the other option, *Let me manage my own virtual memory settings*. Click this option, and specify a minimum setting of 32 Mbyte and a maximum of 100 Mbyte (if your hard drive space permits). Do not tick the box marked *Disable Virtual memory* unless you have a very large memory size, 64 Mbyte or more.

Notes: If you find that switching from one program to another is very slow, with the hard drive working hard, this indicates that your memory is inadequate or that it is being badly used. If you have adequate memory, try saving your data and re-starting Windows. If this improves matters, the fault has been due to a program grabbing memory and refusing to release it.

- On some machines, clicking the *Mail* item in Control Panel can cause a false error message relating to low memory. This is caused by code from a previous Windows 95 installation, and can be ignored.

Modems

Setting up: Many computers nowadays are supplied with a modem fitted and set up. If you fit a modem, internal or external, for yourself, you should use the Control Panel *Add New Hardware* options to ensure that Windows recognises the modem. You can check the settings that have been used by clicking on the *Modem* icon in Control Panel. Use *Modem properties* for the modem itself, and *Dialing Properties* for the dialling configuration.

Fast modems: Some computers come fitted with 56K fast modems, but you may find that you cannot use these at the fastest speed setting. This is because there was until recently no universal agreement on standards, but this has now been achieved as the V90 standard, and if you want a fast modem you should wait until certified V90 types are available. Check also that your Internet Provider uses this standard. In future, increased Internet speed will have to be achieved by using data connections such as ISDN or by other schemes such as are offered by cable TV companies or by electricity companies.

See also **Dial-Up Networking**, **Dialler**

Mouse

General: Unless you are using the **Accessibility options** for mouseless control, Windows 98 demands the use of a mouse. The mouse that was connected to your computer when Windows 98 was installed will be set up correctly, but if you change to another mouse type you will have to use the *Add New Hardware* option of Control Panel (see the **Hardware** entry). You can change many aspects of mouse use, such as the double-click speed and the pointer appearance.

Settings: Open Control Panel from Explorer or from Start — Settings. Click on mouse to show the *Settings* panel with its four tabs. The first tab covers button use. You can set up the mouse for right-handed or left-handed use, but do not assume that if you are left-handed it is better to reverse the mouse buttons. Try it for yourself and see if you prefer it.

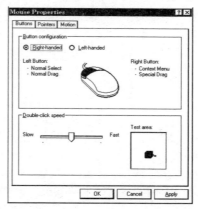

The other part of this panel controls the double-click speed, allowing you to move the slider until your favourite speed of double-clicking will operate the test item, a jack-in-the-box. You can click the *Apply* button to make a change and stay with the panel, or *OK* to make the change and return to Control Panel.

The second tab is marked *Pointers*. The main display shows the pointers that are currently in use for various Windows 98 actions. You can opt to use a *Scheme*, meaning a preset group of pointers, by clicking the arrowhead on this box. The default is usually *None* or *Windows Standard*, with the options of *3D Pointers*, *Animated Hourglasses*, *Windows Standard (Extra Large)* and *Windows Standard (Large)*. If you are worried about the speed of your computer, avoid the 3D and animated effects because they require more work from the processor. You can also select from three sizes for each individual pointer, using the *Browse* button. In this way, you can make up a scheme of your own, using the *Save As* button to preserve your scheme for posterity. You can also, if you want, delete an added scheme.

The third tab is for *Motion*. You can set the speed at any position between *Slow* and *Fast*, and the *Fast* setting is usually preferable for many users. You can also opt to show pointer trails (mouse-tails) which are useful for portable machines with LCD screens (making the pointer movement visible), but not needed on a desktop with a cathode-ray tube monitor. The duration of trails can also be set. Try it for yourself to see if you like a pointer that leaves a trail.

The last tab is *General*, and is used only when you need to change the type of mouse.

Notes: Settings of double-click speed are less important for Windows 98 unless you opt for the classic Windows desktop.

MS-DOS programs

General: MS-DOS programs are older programs, many of them written long before Windows became established (though Windows 98 makes use of the MS-DOS operating system and is in that sense itself an MS-DOS program). Many of these programs can run on the oldest types of PC, allowing only a maximum of 640 Kbyte of RAM, and though most of them can be run inside a window, a few can be used only after quitting Windows altogether. Those that can be used inside a window will allow cut, copy and paste actions between the MS-DOS program and any Windows program. Nowadays, you are likely to use only a few utilities that demand MS-DOS.

- You do, however, need to know the rudiments of MS-DOS to cope with the recovery methods that need to be used if your hard drive fails or if you cannot start Windows for any other reason.

If you are using MS-DOS programs, you need to know how to use the MS-DOS system, and if you are not acquainted with the commands and the way they have to be entered you should consult a good book on MS-DOS such as *BP341 MS-DOS 6 explained*. Note that MS-DOS programs which are capable of altering memory content will usually have to be run by closing down Windows, see later.

MS-DOS Prompt: Click Start — Programs — MS-DOS Prompt. When the MS-DOS window appears, start your MS-DOS program by typing its filename (and full folder path, if it is not in the C:\WINDOWS folder), or alternatively use the CD command to move to the correct folder and then type the program name. All commands are executed when you press the RETURN or ENTER key. Most MS-DOS programs (see below for exceptions) will run in this way and you can switch between the MS-DOS program and Windows programs as if the MS-DOS program were a Windows program. You can move and resize the MS-DOS window, and the icons of the window allow for some useful actions. When you are finished with the MS-DOS program, you can type the command EXIT (and press RETURN) to close the MS-DOS prompt window and return to Windows.

Program options: If an MS-DOS program runs without any apparent problems, you need not worry about the options that appear when you click File — Properties — Program with an MS-DOS program selected in the Explorer display. These are summarised here.

The *Tab* set for an MS-DOS program consists of *General*, *Program*, *Font*, *Memory*, *Screen* and *Misc*. The *General* panel follows the same pattern as for *Folders* or other files. The *Program* panel contains the icon and name of the program, and boxes labelled *Command Line*, *Working Folder*, *Batch File*, *Shortcut Key*, and *Run*. The *Command Line* shows the MS-DOS command that is used to start the program when it is run under MS-DOS. The *Working* (Folder) box shows where the program is located. The *Batch File* entry is seldom used; it can be used to contain the name of a batch file that will be run when this program is started. If a *Shortcut* key (or *hot key*) has been assigned, it will be shown in the next box, and the *Run* box allows you to specify if a program is run full-screen or in a reduced window. This last option is often unavailable and greyed out. The Panel contains an *Advanced* button and a *Change Icon* button (whose action is similar to that of changing the icon for any other file).

The *Advanced* button allows fine-tuning of the way that an MS-DOS program is run. The check boxes are labelled *Prevent MS-DOS Programs from Detecting Windows*, *Suggest MS-DOS Mode as Necessary*, *MS-DOS Mode*, and

Windows 98 assistant

Warn before entering MS-DOS Mode. The *Prevent MS-DOS Programs from Detecting Windows* box can be ticked if the MS-DOS program is one of a small number that normally refuse to run if Windows is detected. *The Suggest MS-DOS Mode as Necessary* box should be ticked, because it allows Windows to decide what needs to be done, and this is always much faster than manual methods. The *MS-DOS Mode* box must be ticked if the program requires all other programs (including Windows) to be shut down before it can be run. If this is done, Windows will restart automatically when the MS-DOS program ends. The last box can be ticked to provide a warning before Windows is closed down.

The options concern the MS-DOS configuration, which is set by the files CONFIG.SYS and AUTOEXEC.BAT. The default is to use the CONFIG.SYS and AUTOEXEC.BAT files that run before Windows is started, but you can opt to specify different versions of these files which can then be edited in the two panels that are provided. A *Configuration* button can be clicked to ensure that a set of options is used each time this program is started.

- Do **not** alter the MS-DOS settings unless you know what you are doing. Consult the book *BP341 MS-DOS 6 Explained* if you need a tutorial on the use of MS-DOS. If you do not use any MS-DOS programs, or if the few that you use run without problems, you can ignore these settings.

The *Font, Memory, Screen* and *Misc.* Tabs will not necessarily contain any options unless the program is one that can make use of such options. The *Font* panel allows you to opt for *Bitmap Fonts Only*, *TrueType Fonts Only*, or *Both Font Types* (the default). You can select font size ranging from 2×4 (pixels) to 12×22, and panels show a *Window Preview* and a *Font Preview*. The *Panel* buttons are

OK, *Cancel* and *Apply*. The *Apply* button will save the changes you have made without leaving the panel.

The *Memory* panel should not be changed unless you know what you are doing. The *Conventional Memory* section allows amounts of *Total Memory* (in the first 640 Kbyte) to be selected, and also the *Initial Environment* memory. The default is to use *Auto*, but you can click the arrowhead to select various amounts of memory from 40 Kbyte upwards. The *Expanded (EMS) Memory* section is valid only if your computer uses EMS memory, very unusual nowadays. The *Details* button can be click to show how to enable this type of memory, which is used only for a few older MS-DOS programs – such programs have now been superseded by Windows versions. The *Extended (XMS) Memory* section will, by default use the *Auto* setting for *Total Memory*, and will have the *HMA* (High Memory Area) box ticked. The last section deals with *MS-DOS Protected Memory (DPMI)* and once again, the *Auto* setting should be used unless you know that some other setting is appropriate. The *Panel* contains *OK*, *Cancel* and *Apply* buttons with the usual meanings.

The *Screen* panel is divided into sections marked *Usage*, *Window* and *Performance*. In the *Usage* section you can opt for *Full Screen* use or a reduced *Window* (the default). The *Initial* setting can be *Default* or you can opt for 25, 43 or 50 line display. The *Window* section has check boxes, ticked by default, for *Display Toolbar* and *Restore Settings on Startup*. These provide, respectively, for a Toolbar to be shown on an MS-DOS window and for the Window settings to be restored when you leave the MS-DOS program. The *Performance* set has boxes ticked for *Fast ROM Emulation* and for *Dynamic Memory Allocation*. If you experience display problems with the MS-DOS program, try removing the tick from the *Fast ROM Emulation* box. If the MS-DOS program **must** be given priority in memory allocation (which is unusual) remove the tick from the *Dynamic Memory Allocation* box.

The *Misc.* set contains a number of check boxes whose default values should not be changed unless you know that they ought to be changed. The *Foreground* item is *Allow Screen Saver*, and can be ticked if you want a Windows screen saver to be used on the MS-DOS Window. The *Mouse* items are *Quick Edit* and *Exclusive Use*. Ticking *Quick Edit* allows you to Cut and Copy by marking with the mouse, as you would for a Windows program. If this box is not ticked, you have to use the Edit — Mark menu item to select text for Cut or Copy actions. The *Exclusive Use* box will allow only the MS-DOS program to use the mouse, so that you will have no mouse pointer in Windows.

The *Background* section contains the *Always Suspend* box, which can be ticked to ensure that the program uses no system resources when it is inactive. The *Termination* section contains *Warn if Still Active*, which will issue a warning if you try to leave a program which is still running. The *Idle Sensitivity* setting can be left at its middle setting, but you can set it to *High* if you want the processor to ignore the program while it is idle, or to *Low* if you want the processor to pay more attention to an idle program.

The *Other* setting is for *Fast Pasting*, which should be ticked by default, though not all programs will allow this action. The last section deals with key combinations (hot keys) which will carry out Windows actions. If the MS-DOS program uses one or more of these key actions, you should remove the tick from the appropriate box or boxes. This will allow the use of that key combination in the MS-DOS program rather than having its normal Windows effect.

Awkward programs: A few MS-DOS programs cannot run normally when Windows is working, and have to be run either before Windows is loaded or after Windows has been closed. If you need to run an MS-DOS program of this type (usually programs which modify memory or hard drive contents), you can use one of the following routines.

When you switch on the computer, keep the left-hand Ctrl key (or the F8 key, depending on your computer) held down. When the menu appears, select *Command Prompt Only*, which will allow you to use MS-DOS (unless your old MS-DOS AUTOEXEC.BAT file contains as its last command the word WIN, which will start Windows). You can leave MS-DOS by typing WIN (and pressing the RETURN key) or restart the computer to enter Windows in a more orderly way.

The other option to run MS-DOS by itself occurs when you shut down, when you are given the option to *Restart the Computer in MS-DOS Mode*. This also allows you the use of MS-DOS exclusively, and you need to restart the computer when you are finished with the MS-DOS program(s) or type WIN (then press the RETURN key) to move to Windows 98.

Notes: There are various options on using specific CONFIG.SYS and/or AUTOEXEC.BAT files for specific MS-DOS programs, but you need some experience and expertise with MS-DOS to be able to use these options, and with the relentless march of Windows there is little point now that all the major programs you are likely to use exist in Windows versions.

Multimedia

General: The multimedia options are designed to allow you to make the most of whatever multimedia devices you have, though if you are only concerned with using software such as *Encarta* you can disregard almost everything except the volume control. Some of the settings, such as for sound recording quality or work with MIDI devices require knowledge and experience that is outside the realms of computing, and no attempt is made here, because of pressure of space, to explain such items. In general, if you don't understand the use of some option you probably don't need it!

Selecting options: Click on Control Panel from Explorer or use Start — Settings — Control Panel. Click the *Multimedia* icon. The panel which appears has five tabs which are explained below. These are labelled *Audio*, *Video*, *MIDI*, *CD Music*, and *Devices*.

Audio tab: This consists of two sections. The *Playback* section deals with the playback of sound and the *Preferred Device* that appears will correspond to your sound card – for example, SB16 Wave Out (220) refers to a 16-bit Sound Blaster card. Though there is an arrowhead on this option, the alternative that appears is usually *Use any available device*, since few stand-alone computers will have a choice of sound cards.

The *Recording* section of this tab is similarly arranged with a *Preferred Device*. The *Preferred Device* will be the *Wave In* section of the sound card, so that for the same Sound Blaster card it would read *SB16 Wave In (220)*.

The option boxes on this pane provide for *Use only preferred devices*, and *Show volume control on the taskbar*, both of which are ticked as defaults.

For both sections, the *Advanced Properties* button leads to other choices. For playback, you can select the type of loudspeakers that you are using, with a default of *Desktop Stereo Speakers*. A Performance tab can be clicked to control *Hardware acceleration* and *Sample rate conversion quality*. These should be left at the default settings unless you have some reason to change them. The *Advanced*

Properties for Recording use the same two factors, also set at *Full* acceleration and *Good* quality.

Video: The *Video* tab is fairly straightforward. You can opt to show a video display in a reduced *Window* or *Full Screen*. If you take the default option of a window, you have several choices on window size, with the default being original size. The other size options are *Double original*, $^{1}/_{16}$ *screen size*, $^{1}/_{4}$ *screen size*, $^{1}/_{2}$ *screen size* and *Maximised*. The defaults of *Window* and *Original* size are sensible, because unless you have a specialised video card which is capable of dealing with larger video images, attempts to show video pictures larger than original size will be very disappointing, with jerky movement and slow drawing of images.

MIDI: This tab is of use only if you are using a MIDI interface to an electronic instrument, and if you know how to use it. If you need information on MIDI, see any of the excellent books on the subject by R. A. Penfold. The default setting is for a single instrument, using *MIDI for Internal OPL2/OPL3 FM Synthesis*, with an option of *MIDI for External MIDI Port*. You can also make a *Custom MIDI Configuration*, setting up a *MIDI scheme* of your own by way of the *Configure* button. There is also an *Add New Instrument* button which leads to a Wizard for installing new hardware.

CD Music: This tab is also simple, with a confirmation of the *CD-ROM drive letter* (usually D unless you have a second CD-ROM drive or a network), and a *Volume Control* setting for use with headphones (plugged into the headphone socket of the CD-ROM drive).

• An option to use digital playback will be greyed out unless you have a drive that can use this feature.

Devices: This tab leads to a display of devices and drivers, a portion of the display that is available from the System icon in Control Panel. In general, the settings will have been made on installation, and should not be changed unless you know that there are problems with a setting.

- See the entry for **Volume Control** for details of setting up and using this facility.

Notes: Most of the tabs in the Multimedia section are concerned with specialised actions such as might be required for video or music editing or music synthesis, and only the volume control is of much applicability to the non-specialised user.

My Computer

General: The My Computer display is an overall view of the main sections of the computer, meaning the drives (hard, floppy and CD-ROM), the Control Panel, Dial-Up Networking, Schedules Tasks, and the printers. It is a useful way of gaining access to drive information, formatting floppies, using Control Panel, etc., and because My Computer is really a format of Explorer, you can alter the display so that it is the same as that of Explorer, making it unnecessary to use both. You can also make a shortcut to My Computer on the Taskbar rather than have to minimise programs to use the shortcut on the Desktop.

Starting: Reduce the size of any windows that are covering the Desktop and click the My Computer icon. You can *Minimise all Windows* by clicking the right-hand mouse button on any vacant portion of the Taskbar and selecting this option. The default My Computer display is as shown in Web page view.

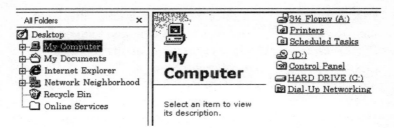

All Folders	×
🗗 Desktop	
⊞ 🖳 My Computer	
⊞ 🗁 My Documents	
⊞ 🌐 Internet Explorer	
⊞ 🖳 Network Neighborhood	
🗑 Recycle Bin	
🗀 Online Services	

My Computer

Select an item to view its description.

- 💾 3½ Floppy (A:)
- 📇 Printers
- 📅 Scheduled Tasks
- 💿 (D:)
- 🎛 Control Panel
- 💽 HARD DRIVE (C:)
- 📠 Dial-Up Networking

Another option for opening My Computer is to click with the right-hand mouse button on the icon in Explorer to see the Quick Menu, and then on *Open*. If you click on *Explore* rather than on *Open*, you will see the My Computer information arranged in the Explorer way, and this latter view can also be obtained by holding down the Shift key and double-clicking the icon. You can also opt to make this the default view, dispensing with the need to use Explorer separately (see below).

- The advantage of using the Explorer type of view is that it has a *Tools* menu with *Find* and *Go To* actions, unlike the default menu of My Computer.

Display options: You can select display options either from the *View* menu or from the Toolbar. The Toolbar can be switched on or off from the *View* menu, and the other display options are *Status Bar*, *Large Icons*, *Small Icons*, *List*, and *Details*. Since the My Computer display is a variation on Explorer, the menu pattern is that of Explorer and the explanations will not be repeated here.

Renaming: If you think that the title My Computer is a trifle tacky, you can edit the name in the usual way – click on it twice (not in quick succession) and then edit. You might like to change the name to *Computer* or the actual model name of your computer. This may have been done for you by the supplier of your computer. Note that you **cannot** rename the Recycle Bin, which is the other main Desktop icon.

Windows 98 assistant

Disc drives: You can click on any disc drive displayed in the My Computer view, so as to select it, and then on File — Properties or on the Properties icon in the Toolbar. Each drive is displayed as its reference letter (such as A:\, C:\) and any label name that has been assigned, see the entry for **Disc names**. The panel which appears shows the disc (for a floppy or CD-ROM) or drive (hard-drive) label name, and you can edit the name in its box. A pie-chart display shows the amounts of used and unused space, with colour codings that are explained. You can click on the *Tools* tab for a report on the three main disc checking actions of *Error checking*, *Backup*, and *Defragmentation*. For each of these headings, you will see a report on how many days have elapsed since the action was carried out, and a button that will start the action of error checking, backup or defragmentation respectively.

Other displays: You can use My Computer for quick access to Control Panel and Printers (which is normally reached through Control Panel). In each case, click to see an Explorer view of the Control Panel or the Printers. You can then click any Control Panel item to run it.

Explore view: You can use the *Options* menu of My Computer to make the Explorer view the default option. Click the View — Options button, then the *File Type* tab. In the list of File Types, move down to folder and click on that name, then on the *Edit* button. The box that appears will have the word **open** in bold print. If the word **explore** also appears, click on it and then on the *Set Default* button. If the word **explore** does not appear, click on the *New* button so that you can type the word **explore** and click the *Browse* button to find the Explorer program in the C:\WINDOWS folder. You can then leave this box so as to select the explore action and make it the default as above. As noted in the entry for Internet Explorer, you can make this the basis for a universal form of Explorer.

Other shortcuts: If you normally work with the Desktop covered, it is very inconvenient to have to start My Computer by minimising all programs, though this can be done quickly by using the right-hand mouse menu. Another useful option is to place a shortcut to My Computer into the Start Menu set. To do this, use Explorer or the Explorer view of My Computer, so that the My Computer folder appears on the right hand side of the display. Click on it and then on File — Create Shortcut. Click on the shortcut so as to select it, and use Edit — Cut. Move to the folder in which you want to place the Shortcut and click the Edit — Paste option. You will see a *Shortcut to* My Computer item appear, allowing you to open My Computer from the Start menu.

Note: If you put a shortcut to My Computer in the *Startup* menu, you may find two copies when you next restart Windows. Like Explorer, My Computer will be automatically restored if it has been running when you switched down Windows, so that it is unnecessary to put it in the *Startup* menu unless you always close it before you switch down.

Notepad

General: Notepad is a simple utility that is used to read, edit, or create ASCII document files of less than 64 Kbyte size. It is usually invoked automatically if you click on a file that carries the TXT extension letters, or it can be opened from the Start — Programs — Accessories menu. Notepad, as the name suggests, is also a convenient way of making short notes and saving them as a file or as a scrap (see entry for **scrap**). There is a more fully-featured version of Notepad available on the Web, and this can be found at:

http://www.cetussoft.com/notepad.htm

This Cnotepad program allows for spelling checks, multiple documents and Print Preview actions, and is a substantial upgrade of the Microsoft Notepad supplied with Windows.

Opening: Click Start — Programs — Accessories and click on the *Notepad* icon. If you make a shortcut in the Startup menu, you can have Notepad started for you automatically when you start Windows. See entry for **Taskbar**.

File menu: The File menu of Notepad consists of the usual *New*, *Open*, *Save* and *Save As* items, along with Page Setup, Print and Exit. *Open* will start a search for files of type TXT, starting in the C:\WINDOWS folder, and with a brief Toolbar that allows you to move up one folder, create a new folder, display as a list or display with full details.

- You can type in a filename if you know what file you want, or opt in the *Files of Type* display for *All Files* rather than just text files – this is useful if you want to use Notepad to edit system files such as CONFIG.SYS or AUTOEXEC.BAT.

The *Save* item will save a file that has previously been opened and allocated a filename, and *Save As* allows you to specify a new name, new location or both, either for an existing file or for a piece of text that you have just created. You need not save a document file with the TXT extension, but using this default makes it much easier to locate such files when you later want to open them.

Page Setup allows you to specify paper size, paper source on the printer, paper orientation as portrait or landscape, margin sizes, plus header and footer text.

The header and footers text uses letter codes prefixed by the ampersand sign (&), with the following meanings:

&f	filename	&d	date
&t	time	&p	page number
&&	& sign	&l, &c, &r	align left, centre, right

Edit menu: The Edit menu contains an *Undo* action which will undo the most recent action, but not a string of actions. The key alternative to the menu is Ctrl-Z. The familiar *Cut*, *Copy* and *Paste* actions are also in this menu. *Cut* (Ctrl-X) will remove selected text from Notepad, and *Copy* (Ctrl-C) will make a copy but not delete the original. *Paste* (Ctrl-V) will paste in cut or copied material (you can open more than one copy of Notepad and paste material from one to another). There is also a *Delete* item, but the use of the Delete key is usually more convenient.

The *Select All* item allows all of the text to be selected without the need to drag the cursor over all of the text, and the *Time/Date* option (F5 key) will place the current Time and Date information into your document at the cursor position. The *Word Wrap* option can be clicked to ensure that lines in Notepad are the same width as the window. You should always use this option when you are viewing files as otherwise you may need to scroll sideways to see the whole of a line. The option is also useful when you are typing because it prevents lines from disappearing beyond the right hand edge of the window.

The *Set Font* item, which was not used in earlier versions of Notepad, allows you to select any font that is present on your computer. The default is a System type of font which looks rather poor in print, and you can now make use of better-looking printer fonts such as Times Roman. The font is displayed and printed, but not saved.

Windows 98 assistant

Search: The *Search* menu item contains only *Find* and *Find Next* (with the F3 key options for *Find Next*). Clicking *Find* produces a small panel which you can use to specify a piece of text that you want to find in your Notepad file. When you have typed this text, another *Find Next* button in the panel is activated, and you can click it to carry out the *Find* action, and subsequent *Find Next* items. You can use the F3 key or the Search — Find Next options if you have closed the *Find* panel. The *Find* panel contains a check box for *Match Case*, and you can opt to search either up or down a document.

Notes: Though Notepad is a text editor, you can open files that are not text files. If you use it to open a program file, for example, you can read any text that is built into the program, and all the program codes will appear as various character shapes. Do not attempt to change and re-save any **program** file with Notepad, because this will almost certainly cripple the program unless you have edited only a portion of text, making changes that do not affect the number of characters in the text.

Windows 98 will automatically make use of Notepad to read text files, but if a file is too large to be read by Notepad it will be read using WordPad.

Objects

General: An *object* is an inserted item in a document, which might be a piece of text from another document, an illustration from Paint or other drawing program, a burst of sound, an animation, a portion of a spreadsheet, or any other extracted material. An imported object can be *embedded* or *linked* into a document. When an object is embedded, it becomes a part of the document and is saved with the document. When the object has been created by a different type of program (as for a drawing embedded in a text document) it can be edited by clicking on the object. This will start the program which created the object, with the object in place to be edited. When an object is linked, its file is connected to your document, but only by a shortcut of a few bytes, so that the size of the document is almost unchanged. To edit the object, you need to run the program that created it, save the altered file, and update the links to your document (for example, use Format — Links in Microsoft Word).

Embed object: The ordinary *Cut* or *Copy* and *Paste* action is an embedding type of action, and you can use this in the normal way. An object can be embedded in this way even if no file copy exists, and some programs, such as Word, allow you to create an object for embedding by starting up a suitable program from a Word instruction. An object can be embedded in more than one document (and into more than one place in a document). If you find that a pasted object cannot be edited by clicking on it, this is because you have pasted it into an application that does not support embedding, or that it is not truly embedded (you might have to use a *Paste Special* command to embed it).

Link object: If an object is to be linked, it must first be created in a suitable program, and saved as a file. It can then be selected and cut or copied, and in the document, pasted in using the *Paste Special* command, and opting for *Paste Link*. If the document is created by a program that does not support linking (rare nowadays) there will be no *Paste Link* command. An object can be linked into more than one document and into more than one place in a document. If you subsequently change the file for the linked object, all the copies that appear in documents will also change. Programs that support linking will allow the editing of links, so that you can update links, or change links to another file.

Windows 98 assistant

Note: Different programs treat these actions differently, and you need to know what variations exist on your own software.

- You can embed or link an object inside another object. For example, in Word you can embed a drawing in a document and have an *Equation* embedded within the drawing.

- Remember that embedded objects can greatly increase the size of a file. Conversely, using linking can cause delays when you are viewing or printing a document.

Outlook Express

General: Outlook Express is the E-mail and News section of Explorer, and is started either from the icon in the Taskbar of Windows 98, or from Internet or Windows Explorer. You must have Internet access in order to use Outlook Express, You will need the name(s) of the Mail and News servers that you use, your account name, and your password. You must specify both an incoming **and** an outgoing mail server. This information is normally supplied by your Internet service provider, or by your system administrator if you are working on a network. The illustration, following, shows the Outlook Express screen organised into sections and reduced to fit this page.

Connections: To make the Mail and News connections, if these have not already been made for you, start Outlook Express and click Tools — Accounts. If no servers appear in the *News* and *Mail* tabs, you will have to add them for yourself, using the information from your IP. Click *Add*, and then the *Mail* or *News* item. This starts the Internet Connection Wizard to add your Mail or News server. You have to deal with Mail and News separately. For example,

Global Net uses the account name of **mail.globalnet.co.uk** for mail and **news.globalnet.co.uk** for news.

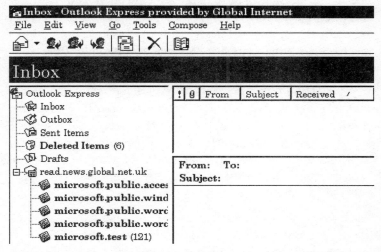

Once this information has been entered, starting Mail will log on to your e-mail account, and download any new messages into your *Inbox* folder. You can switch to News to select newsgroups and to see updated news in your selected groups.

Options: Click on Tools — Options to see the seven tabs labelled *General, Send, Read, Spelling, Security, Dial Up* and *Advanced*. The *General* tab consists of ten option boxes:

Check for new messages every 10 minutes (the time can be altered)
Play sound when new messages arrive
Empty messages from 'Deleted items' folder on exit
Automatically put people I reply to in my Address Book
Make Outlook Express my default email program
Make Outlook Express my default Simple MAPI client
Make Outlook Express my default news reader
When starting, go directly to Inbox folder
Notify me if there are any new Newsgroups

Windows 98 assistant

Automatically display folder with unread messages

These are straightforward, and all can be ticked with the exception of the *MAPI server* item, though you might want to retain the storage of *Deleted Items* because this allows you to check what you have received at some later time.

The *Send* tab consists of format options, which should be left at their default settings unless you have good reason to change them, and a set of five options boxes. The format options are for *Mail* and *News* separately, offering the options of *HTML* (default for Mail) or *Plain Text* (default for News). You may want to change the Mail option to *Plain Text*, because some Mail contacts may be unable to read text in HTML format.

There is a *Settings* button for each option, and you can click this to see the settings, though it is better not to alter the settings unless you have been advised to. For *Plain Text* this provides a default of *Uuencode,* the standard system for encoding and decoding. You can also choose when to wrap text, with a default of 76 characters. If you opt for the alternative MIME system you have a choice for encoding of *None, Quoted Printable*, or *Base 64*, and you can tick a box marked *Allow 8-bit Characters in Header* — this disables encoding for headers. The *HTML* option *Settings* box provides a coding choice of *Quoted Printable* or *Base 64*, and also provides for leaving headers un-encoded.

The check boxes underneath are:

Save copy of sent message in the 'Sent Items' folder
Include message in reply
Send message immediately
Reply to messages using the format in which they were sent
Automatically complete e-mail addresses when composing

You might like to leave the *Send messages immediately* item unchecked, because this allows you to compose a number of messages without going online to send each. This way, the messages can be gathered in the *Outbox* folder and will be sent when you go online or the next time you start Outlook Express online. The other boxes can be ticked, because they are all useful for most purposes.

The *Read* tab is concerned with message reading setting, fonts in received messages and International settings. The first section consists of seven check boxes:

Message is read if previewed for 10 seconds (the time can be changed)
Download 300 headers at a time (number can be changed)
Automatically expand conversation threads
Automatically show new messages in the Preview pane
Mark all messages as read on exiting a newsgroup
Automatically show picture attachments in messages
Show multiple pictures as a slide show

Messages start off unread, and you can distinguish the items you have read from those you have not read by marking. An unread message or group is in **bold** type, and read messages or groups are in plain (Roman) type. You can manually mark messages or groups.

If you want to use manual marking, click Edit — Mark As Read or Edit — Mark as Unread. In News, you can mark a *thread* (an original message and all of the subsequent replies) by clicking on any message in the thread and clicking *Mark Thread As Read*. Another route to marking is to click over the page with the **right-hand** mouse button and then click *Mark as Read, Mark as Unread,* or *Mark Thread as Read* from the menu that appears.

The *Spelling* tab consists of general options and checking options. The general options are:
Always suggest replacement for misspelled word
Always check spelling before sending

and you should check both — a glance at some items you receive will show how badly this facility is needed. The second part of this tab contains four check boxes concerned with items you want to ignore in a spelling check, listed as:

Words in UPPERCASE
Words with numbers
The original text in a reply or forward
Internet addresses

and of these you should certainly tick the last two.

You can use buttons for *Language* and for editing a custom dictionary. The default language will be the one you specified when setting up Windows, and if you use Word, the custom dictionary will be the one that Word uses. When you click the *Edit custom dictionary* button you will see the list of words in Notepad, so that you can add, delete or edit words as you please. You will need to edit if you have unintentionally added a misspelled work to your custom dictionary. Note that you cannot edit the main dictionary.

The *Security* tab consists of *Security Zones*, *Secure Mail* and *Digital Ids*. The default *Security Zone* for mail and news is *Internet Zone*, but you can if you want alter this to *Restricted Sites Zone* for maximum security, since News or Mail can be a source of virus infection. The *Setting* button leads to the same *Security* settings as are used elsewhere in Internet Explorer. In general, you would need only to alter the choice of *Zone* for Mail/News purposes.

There are two *Secure Mail* options, useable only if your correspondents also use mail security:

Digitally sign all outgoing messages
Encrypt contents and attachments for all outgoing messages

Using the digital signature is an assurance to a recipient that your messages is authentic, and the encryption option makes the message difficult to read by an outsider. The *Advanced*

Settings button allows you to specify whether or not to send the private part of your *Digital ID* with the message (so that the recipient can reply using the same coding) or to use another form of encryption called PKCS# signedData. The last portion of the tab allows you to send for a *Digital ID* online, and to obtain more information about the system. In general, you will need this system only if your correspondence is confidential (more so than telephone or post), and if your correspondents use the system.

The *Dial Up* tab items are normally greyed out when you work through Internet Explorer. If you are using Outlook Express by itself, the options are:

Do not dial a connection
Dial this connection (box for specifying connection)
Ask me if I would like to dial a connection

and there are check boxes for

Warn me before switching dial up connection
Hang up when finished sending, receiving or downloading
Automatically dial when checking for new messages

The *Advanced* tab is concerned with retaining news messages, and with maintaining log files (for troubleshooting purposes). The *Local Message* files section has check boxes:

Delete messages 30 days after being downloaded (the number can be changed)
Don't keep read messages

and there is a *Clean Up Now* button to delete files if you have not used automatic deletion, or if you feel that your system is getting too cluttered. Finally, the *Logging* options are listed as:

News transport
Mail transport
IMAP transport

Windows 98 assistant

IMAP is a form of mail server that allows messages to be stored and retrieved from more than one computer. You can also opt to use storage on the default POP3 system by clicking Accounts — Options — Advanced — Delivery

Display: The default display of Outlook Express uses a folders/files tree, a pane for headers, and a preview pane. The *Preview Pane* is used to indicate the complete content of a message. You can alter the default view of Outlook Express using View — Layout. The first section consists of four options:

Outlook bar   Folders list   Folder Bar   Tip of the Day

and the default choice is *Folders list* and *Tip of the Day*. You might prefer the view given by clearing these and ticking the other two.

The second part of Layout concerns Toolbar display, with option buttons for *Top*, *Left*, *Bottom* or *Right*. There is also a check box for *Show text on toolbar button*, which is ticked by default. The *Customize Toolbar* button allows you to add buttons (such as Address Book) or to remove buttons (such as *Drafts*).

The last portion deals with the *Preview Pane*. There is a checkbox, ticked by default, to use the preview pane, and there are option buttons for placing the *Preview Pane* below or beside the *Messages* list. You can also drag the divider between the preview pane and the message list. You can also use another check box to determine whether or not you want a header on the preview pane. Since the information for the header is present in the message list, clearing this box makes the display less cluttered.

Receiving messages: You can select an automatic option for receiving mail/news, or you can use a menu action. When messages are received they are stored in a folder and can be read or printed. To use the automatic option, Click

Tools — Options — General and select the check box marked *Check for new messages every 10 minutes*. Alter the time setting to suit your needs. With this box ticked, Outlook Express will also check for incoming messages each time you start up. For manual checking, click Tools — Send And Receive. Make sure that the *Inbox* is selected in your folders list or Outlook bar.

Click the message in the message list to read the message in the *Preview Pane*. If a message comes with an attachment, click the file attachment icon in the preview pane and then click the filename. You can copy or move the message — right-click on the message header and select *Move To* or *Copy To*. You can also select Print if you want to print the message. You can also use the menu items File — Print or Edit — Copy.

To forward a received message to someone else, open the message, and use the *Forward Message* icon on the toolbar. An alternative is to click over the message with the **right-hand** mouse button and then click *Forward* from the menu that appears. You will need to type the e-mail address for each recipient (separate addresses with semicolons). Type any accompanying message, then click the *Send* button on the toolbar.

You can automatically mark messages as read or unread. Click Tools — Options — Read, and click the check box labelled *Message is Read After Being Previewed for 5 Seconds*. Fill in the time you want to use. For newsgroups you can tick the item labelled *Mark all messages as read when exiting a newsgroup*.

If you want to use manual marking, click Edit — Mark As Read or Edit — Mark as Unread. You can also use *Mark All as Read*.

Windows 98 assistant

For News messages, you can mark a thread (original message and all subsequent replies) by clicking on any message in the thread and clicking *Mark Thread As Read*. Another route to marking is to click over the page with the **right-hand** mouse button and then click *Mark Thread as Read* from the menu that appears. To display properties for a message, right-click the name.

- Incoming mail that has priority is distinguished by the exclamation mark icon in the message list.

- Incoming mail that uses HTML is marked by using bold type for the header.

Sending messages: Mail is addressed to a recipient, and you can type the e-mail name or take it from the *Address Book* (see later), and you can also send to more than one recipient. You can also send copies of mail to other recipients using the *Cc* (carbon copy) and Bcc (blind carbon copy) boxes, and you can reply to mail, with the original letter on the same page.

To send a new message, Click *Compose Message* and type the e-mail name of the recipient into the *To* box. If you have Address Book organised, you can click on the letter icon to see a list of names (which are converted to e-mail format automatically). If you want to send to more than one recipient, separate the names by a semicolons. Fill in a *Subject*, type in or paste your message, and click File — Send Message or Send Later.

- Note that there is an arrowhead next to the Compose Message button. This can be clicked to see a set of standard messages such as party invitations.

If you are replying to an incoming message, click the message that you want to reply to in the message list. Click the *Reply to Author* button in the toolbar, or click over the message with the **right-hand** mouse button and then click *Reply to Author* from the menu that appears.

You can add other names in the *To, Cc* or *Bcc* boxes (use semicolons to separate names). If you want to add names from the *Address Book*, click the *Address Book* icon on the toolbar and click a name you want to add. Type the message and use the Send and Receive button. See later for more details of the *Address Book*.

You can alter the priority of outgoing Mail messages at the time you compose the mail, so that when the messages are transmitted they will be in priority order. You cannot change the priority of outgoing News messages. Click Tools — Set Priority, and then select *High, Normal* or *Low*. Note that this item is not available when the message is sent to the *Outbox*.

Once a message has been sent to the *Outbox* you can view it, but you cannot edit it. If you have second thoughts, move the item into the *Drafts* box, edit it there and copy the text. Start a new message and paste in your edited copy. This new version can then be sent to the *Outbox*.

Address book: Outlook Express can use the *Address Book* for both e-mail contacts and newsgroups. You can then use this data to make contacts, and you can edit the information as and when required. To add e-mail contacts, click on Address Book — New contact, and select which group your contact belongs to. The choice is of *Personal, Home, Business, Other* and *Conferencing*, and there is an additional tab for *Digital IDs* for contacts that must be secure. When you select a group, you can then type the information required (typically name, nickname, e-mail address, phone numbers for e-mail contact). For a Newsgroup, you first type *Group name*, and you can then type the details for each *Members* you add. You can also add the name of someone who has sent you a message to the appropriate *Address book* section when you are viewing a message — click the name with the **right-hand** mouse button and then click the *Add to Address Book* option. Note that the name you type can be a nickname or an *alias* rather than the full name or the e-mail name.

- You can opt automatically to add the name on each message you reply to into your Address Book. Use Tools — Options — General and tick the box marked *Automatically put people I reply to in my Address Book*.

You can edit any address book entry by right-clicking it and clicking on *Properties* from the menu that appears. This allows you to change any part of the stored information, or to delete the whole entry by clicking on *Delete* instead of on *Properties*.

If you use a *Windows Messaging Personal Address Book* (not the same as the Mail/News *Address Book*), click File — Import — Address Book and then click *Options* to choose how you want to select names (which might not be in e-mail format).

Properties: The *Properties* item of the File menu in Outlook Express can be used to find information on any received message. An alternative route to this is to click the message using the **right-hand** mouse button, and then select *Properties* from the menu that appears. The *Properties* pane has normally two tabs, labelled *General* and *Details*.

The General pane contains information on *Subject, From, Size, Location, Attachment, Attachment Format, Priority, Sent date/time* and *Received date/time*. One or more of these may be blank if it does not apply. The *Details* pane shows the Headers for the message. A button marked *Message Source* will use Notepad to display the HTML source code for the message.

Sorting messages: You can sort messages into order, using the headings of *Priority, Attachment, From* (name), *Subject* and *Received* (date). The sort can be ascending or descending. For News in particular there is an additional option of *Group Messages by Subject*. To sort, click View — Sort By and make your choice of topic. Only the *Ascending* option appears in the list, but if the tick is not visible against *Ascending*, the sort is descending.

E-mail folders: When you install Outlook Express, data files called *Deleted Items, Draft, Inbox, Outbox,* and *Sent items* are created. You **cannot** delete these files in any normal way, but you can add other files to this set. You should not attempt to alter these files using Windows Explorer because if you do so they can become corrupted and unusable. You can add a folder by clicking File — Folder — New Folder. Select the folder for which your new folder will be a sub-folder and then type a name for your new folder in the *Name* box and click OK. You can delete a folder **that you have created**, by selecting the folder and using File — Folder — Delete. Remember that you should not attempt to delete any of the default folders. Another folder action is compacting, using File — Folder — Compact or Compact All Folders. Compacting folders saves hard drive space.

The *Inbox* contains a message when you go online and receive a message. You will normally read the message and then delete it. This moves the message to the *Deleted Items* box. Messages will remain in the Inbox until you delete them. The *Outbox* is used to store messages that are sent out. You can opt to send immediately, or only when instructed. This way, you can compose offline and send only when you are ready, without running up telephone charges while you are typing.

When you delete a message from the message list, the message is held in a *Deleted Items* folder. You can empty this folder by selecting all the messages and using the Delete key or Edit — Delete. This permanently deletes the files, so that you cannot use the *Copy To* or *Move To* commands to recover the 'deleted' files into another folder. You will be prompted to confirm the deletion. In this respect, the *Deleted Items* folder and *Sent Items* folder act like the Recycle Bin of Windows 98. For automatic deletion, you can use the Tools — Options General pane to tick the check box for *Empty Messages from 'Deleted Items' folder on exiting*. If you want to recycle a deleted message, move it first to the *Drafts* box.

Items in the *Sent Items* folder can be deleted in the same way, but you are not prompted to confirm. You can opt for deleting news messages after a time, using Tools — Options — Advanced. You can avoid using the *Sent Items* folder if you remove the tick from *Save Copy Of Sent Messages In The 'Sent Items' Folder* in the Tools — Options — Send pane.

- If you do not normally save copies of outgoing messages, you can type your own e-mail address into the *Cc* box to make a copy of that message when it is sent.

Copy and move: You can copy or move messages to the data folders by clicking the message and use Edit — Move To Folder or Copy To Folder, then click the folder on the list that appears. Another route is to click over the page with the **right-hand** mouse button and then click *Move To* or *Copy To* from the menu that appears. If you want to copy a message to another document, use Edit — Copy and then paste into the other document. You can also select text in a message, right-click it and select *Copy* to paste in the selected text.

The File *Import* and *Export* options are for use with other messaging systems, and you can use them if you are changing over to Outlook Express from an older system.

Inbox assistant: This allows you to specify filtering for your incoming mail, so that only mail from approved sources is placed in the *Inbox*. When you click on this item, you will see a pane that contains a blank area titles *Description*. To make use of this, click the *Add* button, and you will see a panel that consists of two parts, criteria for messages, and what to do with messages that fulfil the criteria. The Criteria section consists of checkboxes for:

All messages, To, CC, From, Subject, Account, and *Larger than*.

and the action set consists of :

Move To, Copy To, Forward To, Reply With, Do not download from Server and *Delete off server*.

This allows you, for example, to refuse mail or news from some sources or to put mail relating to some subjects straight into the *Deleted Items* folder (using Move To) This facility allows you to deal with junk email and prevents more coming from the same source.

News: You switch to News in Outlook Express by clicking on the News icon, or by using the Go — News menu. A News message will appear automatically in the *Preview Pane* unless you disable the Auto download action. Click Tools — Options — Read, then clear the check box marked *Automatically show News messages in Preview Pane*. If you decide that you want to see the message, you can select the message and press the Spacebar.

You can search for newsgroups while you are online with News running by clicking the *Newsgroups* button. Click the newsgroup(s) you want to see or subscribe to in the list that appears, then click the *Subscribe* button. You can search for names by typing it into the box labelled *Display newsgroups which contain*. If you cannot find a newsgroup that you know exists (having read the name in a printed list), try another server. To remove your subscription, click the Newsgroup in the list and then click the *Unsubscribe* button.

- Remember that subscribing to a Newsgroup does not necessarily require money to be paid, it simply registers your interest so that you will be notified when new messages are available.

The Newsgroup list allows you viewing options of *All*, *Subscribed* and *New*, to make searching easier. If you find that there are newsgroups whose titles are offensive (and be in no doubt that some are) you can use Tools — Filter Newsgroups to set criteria for these groups appearing. Click the *Add* button, and type your criteria of words that you do not want to see.

The default is to download 300 headers for each newsgroup. You can alter this to a different value or remove the cross from the check box, in which case all the headers in the group will be downloaded. This may amount to considerably more than 500 if you are viewing a popular group.

By its nature, News will place large files of data onto your hard drive. Each Newsgroup keeps its own memory cache on your computer so that you do not need to download all of the information each time you connect, only the items that have changed. The normal action is that old messages and headers are removed (purged) at intervals. You can gain disc space by purging large cache files at intervals if you do not need them. Click on Options — Advanced. To enforce a purge after a stated time, click on the box marked *Delete message 5 days after downloading* and edit the time interval (up to 999 days) as required. You might also want to tick the box marked *Don't keep read messages* so that only the messages that you have not read are stored. Another option is *Compact file when there is 20% wasted space*, and you can determine the percentage for yourself. You can enforce a purge directly by clicking on the *Clean Up Now* button.

This will offer options of compacting, deleting text (leaving headers) or deleting completely. There is also an option for recovering news data when you are online.

Marking newsgroups: You can mark the newsgroups you want to download before making connection, so saving valuable telephone time. The marking method allows you to select all of the newsgroups you subscribe to, or a selection (which can include newsgroups you do not subscribe to). While you are offline, select newsgroups from the list (News groups button) and click Tools — Mark for retrieval — All messages (or you can opt for *New headers*). When you have marked newsgroups offline, click the Tools — Download All menu to go online and download the news.

Threads: A thread consists of an original document and all the replies (and replies to replies...) that it generates. The name *thread* is used because the documents are connected, they have a common thread running through them. Very often you will want to download all the messages in a thread so that you can read the arguments after you have gone offline. You can opt to download a complete thread or individual messages.

The message list contains icons that are used to mark threads. The + icon can be clicked to expand a thread and show all messages, the – icon can be clicked to collapse the list to the title of the original message. If only the first message of a thread is visible, click on the [+] icon in the message list or use View — Expand to see all the messages in a thread. If you want to see the original message only, click on the [–] icon or use View — Collapse.

You can select items in the message list for downloading. You can select threads or individual messages as you please. Hold down the Ctrl key if you want to select more than one item. When you have marked your messages, click Tools — Download this newsgroup. You can opt to download all of the messages in a thread. Use Tools — Options — Read — Automatically expand conversation threads.

Messages that are downloaded are automatically marked as unread, and the distinction between read and unread messages is important — for example you can use the Ctrl–U keys to see the next unread message. You can manually mark messages as read (or as unread even if you have read them), using the *Mark* commands in the *Edit* menu. In this menu also you can mark a thread as read. You can opt to have all messages automatically marked as read if you preview them for at least a specified time, default 5 seconds. To alter this, click on Tools — Options — Read and tick the check box labelled *Message is Read After Being Previewed for 5 Seconds*. You can clear the box, so that all messages have to marked manually after you have read them, or you can alter the time setting to one that gives you time to read a long message.

Answering messages: You can use a Newsgroup entirely passively, viewing messages without replying to them, or you can send reply messages on an individual or a group basis. Click the message, and then use one of the toolbar buttons such as *Reply to Group*, *Reply to Author* or *Forward Message*. An alternative is to click over the page with the **right-hand** mouse button and then click *Reply to Newsgroup* from the menu that appears.

You can reply to one Newsgroup, or type the names of several Newsgroups, using a semicolon to separate the names. You must type the subject of your message. When you have typed the message, click File — Post Message. If you post to more than one Newsgroup, all of the groups must use the same server, otherwise you will need to post a reply for each server that groups belong to.

The Unscramble (ROT13) command of the *Edit* menu puts into readable text form material which has been scrambled by using the ROT13 system, in which each character is replaced by one 13 places on. Material which might be offensive or which you might otherwise not want to see (plot of next month's soap, for example) is sometimes encoded in this way. Do not confuse ROT13 text with Cyrillic text that appears converted to a Western font.

Paint

General: Paint is the Windows 95/98 graphics painting program that replaces the Paintbrush program of Windows 3.1. Many users preferred Paintbrush, particularly for its ability to create the compact PCX type of data files, and for better cursor control, and so use the older program rather than its replacement. The new version now includes the compact JPEG and GIF formats for graphics files.

Paint, like WordPad, is a fairly substantial program in its own right, and would require a book of about this size again for a really full treatment, so that what follows is only an outline guide. The Windows 98 version is only slightly changed from the Windows 95 version.

Starting Paint: Click Start — Programs — Accessories — Paint. The Paint window will appear and should be maximised if you want to create a drawing. The icons are illustrated and named in the illustration following.

Colours: Click on a colour from the palette using the left-hand mouse button to make this the foreground (drawing) colour. Click on a colour with the right-hand mouse button and then click on Image — Clear Image to make this the background colour. If you click a colour with the right-hand mouse button and do not use the *Clear Image* command, this colour will be used only for filling closed shapes (*Fill colour*).

Windows 98 assistant

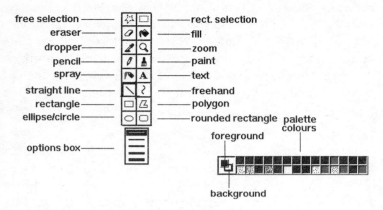

Drawing shapes: Click on the drawing tool and drag the cursor to draw the corresponding shape. The freehand line must be drawn with precise mouse movements, but other shapes can be controlled by using the Shift key. Drawing a straight line with the Shift key held down will make the line perfectly horizontal, vertical, or at 45°, depending on the direction of dragging. Drawing a rectangle with the Shift key held down will create a perfect square, and drawing an ellipse with the Shift key held down will draw a perfect circle.

You can draw a closed shape in outline, with a fill, or consisting of a fill only with no outline, according to your selection from the *Options box* at the left-hand side. The same box will provide a set of line thickness options when a line tool is selected (and other options for other actions). If you want to draw a closed shape with a thick line boundary, select the line thickness **before** you select the closed shape tool. The paintbrush tool uses the options box to provide a set of brush shape and size options, and the spray-gun tool can use a set of spray patterns. The eraser options are for size, and the magnifier options are zoom sizes. Text and selection tools can use the options box to select positioning in front of other objects or behind them.

Selecting and altering: Any drawn shape can be selected using one or other of the selection tools. The rectangular selection tool allows you to draw a perfect rectangle around the area that you want to select, and carry out any permitted action on the enclosed area. The freehand selection tool allows you to define the shape of a selected object more closely as you drag the mouse, though the selection outline appears as a rectangle when you release the mouse button.

On a selected object, the actions that you can carry out are *Moving*, *Copying*, *Deleting*, *Flipping*, *Rotating*, *Stretching*, *Skewing* and *Colour Inversion*. Moving is done by dragging the selected area with the four-arrow icon visible. Copying can be done by dragging with the Ctrl key hold down or by using *Copy* and *Paste* from the Edit menu. Deleting requires you to press the Delete key, the Ctrl-X keys, or the Edit — Clear Selection menu action.

The other effects are reached either through the *Image* menu or by using Ctrl-key combinations. Image — Flip/Rotate (Ctrl-R) will produce a panel with the options of *Flip horizontally*, *Flip vertically*, or *Rotate*, with a choice of 90°, 180° and 270° angles. The *Stretch/Skew* menu choice (Ctrl-W) shows a panel with *Horizontal* and *Vertical* options for the *Stretch* action, each with a percentage panel into which you can enter the percentage stretch amount. The *Skew* portion of the panel allows for *Horizontal* or *Vertical* skew, with the amount specified in degrees. The *Invert Colour* choice (Ctrl-I) will reverse the foreground and background colours, and this action shows up very clearly the difference between a rectangular selection and a freehand selection.

Image attributes provides information on a drawing, showing the width and height, measuring units, colours and if transparent background colours have been used.

The text tool allows text, with the usual options of fonts and sizes, to be added to a picture. If you click View — Text

Windows 98 assistant

Toolbar you will see a toolbar appear that allows easy choice of *Font*, *Size*, and effects (*Bold*, *Italic* and *Underline*). When you click the *Text* tool, you can draw a *Text Box*, and when the cursor appears, you can type your text which will fill the box. You can edit the text or re-size the box until it fits your text, and then click outside the box to remove the box and leave the text. The text will appear either hiding the drawing under it or superimposed, depending on your setting of the *Options box* icons.

Measurements: Paint is not intended for making scale drawings, which is the task of a CAD program (try AutoSketch if you need full CAD facilities in a package that is compatible with AutoCAD but much easier to use). Measurements are indicated on the status bar of Paint, with the cursor position indicated in units of Pixels (*Pels*), and a box measurement indicator that show the size of a closed shape or selection box while you are drawing it (but not after you have released the mouse button). Note that though you can specify units in the Image — Attributes menu, only the pel units are shown on the status bar.

Colours: The basic colour palette of Paint contains 28 colours if you are using a 16-colour display (some 'colours' are patterns), and larger amounts if you are using a 256-colour (or higher) screen. You can use the Options — Edit Colors menu to select from a larger number (48 for the 16-colour screen) or to make your own (*Custom*) colours. Click on a colour in the *Palette*, then on Options — Edit Color. You can click on a colour in the larger colour box in this panel (then on the *OK* button) to place this colour into the *Palette*, replacing the original colour, or you can click the *Custom Color* button to create your own colour by clicking on the colour display that appears in an extension of the panel.

If you create *Custom Colors*, you can save your new colour set as a PAL (palette) file using Options — Save Colors, and you can subsequently load this or any other saved colour set by using the Options — Get Colors menu item. The last item in the *Options* menu is *Draw Opaque* which can be ticked to prevent a selected item showing any item that it covers. If the tick is removed, the underlying item becomes visible. This is the same action as is carried out by the icon pair in the options box when a selection action is being used.

File menu: The *File* menu of Paint contains the usual items of *New*, *Open*, *Save* and *Save As* which carry out the same actions as have been described for other programs. The Open command allows the choice for *Files of Type* of *Bitmap files* (the default), *JPEG files*, *GIF*, *All Picture Files* (not including PCX) or *All Files*. *All Files* displays all files, but allows only compatible files to be opened. You can open PCX files using this option.

The *Save As* command allows the use of *Save as type* consisting of *Monochrome Bitmap*, *16-colour Bitmap*, *256-colour Bitmap*, *24-bit Bitmap*, *JPEG*, or *GIF*.

• Windows 98 allows you to save and open files in the GIF or JPG formats, but only if you have the graphics filter programs of Office 97 installed (in Word 97, for example). Note that JPG is a lossy format — if you load a JPG file, edit it, and then save it again there will be some loss of content.

The second section of the *File* menu contains *Print Preview*, *Page Setup* and *Print*. The *Print Preview* produces a view of the printed page with your drawing in place to show how the page will appear. If you have more than one drawing on separate pages you can use the *Next Page* and *Prev. Page* buttons to look at different drawings, also a *Two Page* option to see two pages on screen, and there is a *Print* button if you want to print without returning to the main menu. The *Page Setup* item will show a page diagram, with boxes for *Paper Size*, option buttons for *Orientation* (*Portrait* or *Landscape*), and *Margins*, with a default value of 0.75" for *Left*, *Right*, *Top* and *Bottom* margin. The last item in this set is *Print*, which will print the drawing using the values in *Page Setup*.

The *Send* item of the *File* menu allows a drawing in Paint to be transmitted by e-mail or Fax, providing that you have set up *Microsoft Exchange*. Note that this is not the same as the Windows 98 *Send To* command which allows a file to be sent to a destination determined by the contents of a folder, see the **Send To** entry.

There are two *Set* items, labelled as *Set as Wallpaper (Tiled)* and *Set as Wallpaper (Centered)* which allow an image to be used as a Desktop wallpaper (see **Desktop** entry). These commands allow you to prepare Wallpaper of your own design.

Finally, the *File List* in the *File* menu is of recently-used files, allowing you to recall any of these files rapidly with a single click.

Edit menu: The Edit menu contains an *Undo* (Ctrl-Z) item, allowing you to reverse up to three of the most recent actions. There is also a *Repeat* (F4) item which will reverse an Undo. The usual set of *Cut* (Ctrl-X), *Copy* (Ctrl-C) and *Paste* (Ctrl-V) follow, and there are also the *Clear Selection* and *Select All* options.

The last two *Edit* menu items are particularly useful. *Copy To* allows a selected portion of an image to be saved to a file for which you can specify a filename and type, and a folder location. This is a form of Crop command. The other command, *Paste From*, carries out the opposite action of pasting an image from a file into a selection box that you can place anywhere on your page. You can, if you want, create the selection box first, but this will not alter the scale of the image so that it fills the box – the selection box will alter size so as to suit the image.

View menu: The View menu contains *Toolbox*, *Color Box*, *Status Bar*, *Text Toolbar, Zoom, View Bitmap* and *Show Thumbnail*. The first four items are selected on (ticked) by default, but you can remove them if you prefer. Clicking on the *Zoom* item produces the choice of *Normal* (Ctrl-Page Up), *Large* (Ctrl-Page Down) or *Custom*, and the *Custom* item can be clicked to allow the selection of 100%, 200%, 400%, 600% or 800%. When a magnification of 400% or more is used, you can click *Show Grid* to display a grid that shows pixels, and you can then edit a shape one pixel at a time, or use the drawing tools on the enlarged view (which is often quicker). The *Show Thumbnail* option in this set will show a small copy of the main picture so that you can see the result of editing on pixels.

The *View Bitmap* item allows you to see your image uncluttered by toolbars, and clicking anywhere in the image area will return you to normal view. The last option is to turn the *Text Toolbar* on or off.

Image Attributes: The other *Image* menu items have already been mentioned. *Image Attributes* allows you to alter the size of the picture outline, the units in which this is stated, and the option of colour or monochrome. Altering size is one method of cropping an image, though it is not so useful as using *Copy To* (with an area selected) or the action of cropping in another document (such as a Word document). Your units choice is inches, centimetres or pels (pixels).

Notes: Unlike Paintbrush which allowed you to move a selection pixel by pixel using the cursor keys (with the mouse button held down), Paint has no way of allowing such precision of movement, and you should reduce the sensitivity of the mouse (using the Mouse item in Control Panel) if you want to carry out such actions.

- Unlike Paintbrush, Paint allows you to change *Image Attributes* without clearing the image.

Passwords

General: Passwords are used mainly by users of machines on a network, which is a set of topics that is not covered in this book. Solo users need not use passwords except for such actions as page ratings, see **Security**, and will find that all of the passwording options described in the Help pages are inapplicable when there is no network fitted. Where the use of a password is permitted with Windows 98 used alone, you should either ignore the provision, or use a password that you can remember but which no-one else can guess. One useful tip is to make a word out of the initial letters of a line of a poem or a song.

Paste special

General: The *Paste Special* command is used mainly for linking files, and the options that appear in the *Paste Special* pane will depend on the nature of the object (picture, text, spreadsheet, etc.) that you are linking.

Picture: For a picture, the options are usually *Picture*, *Bitmap*, *Device independent bitmap* (DIB) and *Picture* (*enhanced metafile*). For the first three options you can select whether or not to float the inserted picture over text, but this option is not available for the enhanced metafile format. The other options of *Paste Link* and *Paste as Icon* will be greyed out if they are not supported by the application that created the picture. *Paste as Icon* is available only if *Paste Link* has been selected. Note that *Paste Link* will not be available unless you are pasting from the application that **originally** created the picture. For example, if you create a picture in Paint and then use Paint Shop Pro to convert it into PCX format and save it, the *Paste Link* action will be greyed out. In general, if you do not see the source of the file stated on the *Paste Special* pane, *Paste Link* will not be available.

Text: Typical options for *Paste Special* with text include the source of the document such as *Word Document Object*, *Formatted text*, *Unformatted text* and *Picture*. You are more likely to find the *Link* and *Icon* options available in this set.

Performance

General: The performance of your computer is ultimately restricted by the type of microprocessor chip and clock speed, amount of memory, hard disc size and organisation and other built-in factors, and there are several steps that you can take to ensure that your programs run as fast as is possible on your system. Windows 98 will help in cutting down the time needed to load your favourite programs, but this is not accomplished at once because it depends on the use of the defragmentation routine over a period.

Chip: If your computer uses a Pentium chip, consider an upgraded faster Pentium, either of the MMX type or Pentium-2 if a suitable upgrade is available. Most Pentium chips (old or MMX) fit the Socket-7, so that on many motherboards it is easy to insert a faster chip if the motherboard supports it. The Pentium-2 chip uses a different socket, and you cannot plug a Pentium-2 into a Socket-7.

Memory: Your computer should be fitted with as much RAM memory as you can afford. There is no substitute, but it is debatable whether fitting more than 64 Mbyte of RAM

Windows 98 assistant

is beneficial at present. Avoid software that claims to offer the benefits of more memory.

Hard drive: The hard drive should be a fast type, and of adequate size – the usual minimum size at the time of writing is 2 Gbyte. A modern hard drive will support Ultra DMA, and unless this is done automatically you may have to tick the DMA box that appears when the Control Panel — System has been clicked, allowing you to click *Device Manager* and then the *Disk Drives* tab. Select the hard drive, and click on the Properties button, then on the Settings tab. If the DMA box is empty, click on it to place a cross in it. If the box is greyed out, it does not necessarily mean that DMA is impossible, it may simply be applied without being notified to Windows in this way.

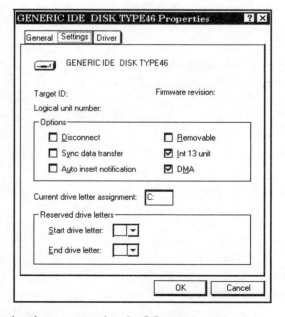

Organisation: see under the **Memory** entry.

Pictures

General: Pictures used in Windows 98 applications will be either of the bitmap or the vector (sometimes called object-oriented) type. The bitmap type is simpler and exists in a large variety of formats, many of which are available in the Paint type of programs. The vector type offers higher quality, particularly if you need to alter the size of the picture. These are used for drawing programs in which precise scale is important. Either type can be stored and pasted in the Windows metafile (WMF) format.

Bitmap: A bitmap is a list of points on the screen with the colour and brightness of each specified. The simple Windows bitmap type of picture takes up a large amount of memory or disc space, but this is the main format that Windows Paint uses, with GIF and JPG available under certain conditions. The PCX type of file, which takes up much less space, can be **loaded** by Paint but not saved in this form. The well-known Corel Paint program will work with bitmaps of various formats, and the excellent Paint Shop Pro is ideal for changing formats, and now has some drawing capabilities

Vector: Vector files are created by drawing applications such as DrawPlus, Corel Draw! and SmartSketch. Pictures are represented by sets of drawing instructions. All vector pictures will display at the maximum resolution permitted by the screen or printer. Vector files can be converted easily to bitmap (import into a bitmap application), but the conversion in the opposite direction is much more difficult, often resulting in unsatisfactory images or very large files or both.

Lossy files: Some image files, such as JPEG, are lossy, meaning that the file size is compressed by losing some of the detail. This may not be important if the file is opened and printed, but re-saving an edited file may result in an unacceptable loss of detail. JPEG picture files are used widely on the Internet because of their small size.

Note: SmartSketch, which is the easiest of all vector drawing programs to use, was at one time on sale in the UK, but can now only be obtained through the Web site:

http://www.futurewave.com.au/smartsketchtrial.htm

and though the current version is for Windows 3.1 (but works on Windows 95), a new version is expected for Windows 95/98.

Plug and Play hardware

General: Hardware additions to your computer should by now all be of the Plug and Play type, meaning that they contain stored information on installation that Windows 98 can act upon. This makes the installation of such hardware literally plug in and use, as distinct from the routine of adjusting jumpers and configuring software that was needed for older hardware.

Installation: With the computer switched off, connect the new hardware, making certain that all plugs are firmly inserted and, where appropriate, locked into place, and any inserted cards screwed down into position. Replace the covers on the machine (unless the hardware has been connected through a port), and switch on. When Windows is running, start Control Panel from Explorer or from Start — Settings, and click on *Add New Hardware*. Follow the instructions, allowing Windows to detect the new hardware automatically. See the **Hardware (add)** entry for details

Notes: Older hardware may need driver software to be read from a floppy, but you should use the *Add New Hardware* routine and try for auto-detection before assuming that manual installation will be needed. Some older hardware still comes with instruction for installation under Windows 3.1, but it should be possible to make a satisfactory installation under Windows 98 — consult the hardware manufacturer (preferably from their Web site) if you are in doubt.

If old hardware comes with a leaflet detailing jumper settings for items called IRQ and DMA you should always consult the manufacturer because you may have difficulties in installing such hardware on a modern Plug and Play computer.

Printing

General: The aim of creating documents is to print them, so that the setup and use of the printer is a very important part of Windows 98. Remember, however, that the program that you are running will to a considerable extent determine how you use the printer, and if you are running a DOS program it must contain its own printer drivers because DOS programs cannot make use of the Windows drivers.

If you want to be able to use printers that are not connected to your system (either directly or mapped through a network) you can install such printers and opt to create a disc of printer codes so that your documents can be printed from this disc by using an MS-DOS command on another computer that is equipped with the desired printer.

Printers: Click Start — Settings — Printers or click the *Printers* icon in the Control Panel. The *Printers* window will open, showing in icon form all the printers (possibly only one) that are installed on your system. As noted above, you may want to install some printers that are not available to your own system. To do this, click the *Add Printer* icon to start a Wizard which will take you through the necessary steps. When you come to specify a *Port*, use the *File:* option if you do not have the printer connected. The same Wizard is used if you want to change to another printer connected to your system, specifying the normal printer port *LPT1* or the alternative *LPT2* if one is fitted.

Printer Setup: Programs that use the printer will all provide for setting up the printer for their own purposes, but the methods can vary. Some will provide a File — Printer Setup menu, others will allow *Setup* actions from File — Print. For example, *Word* uses File — Print to display a panel which has a *Properties* button for setting up the printer (as distinct from items such as page range, number of copies, etc.), and *Notepad* uses its *Page Setup*, again with a *Properties* button.

A more extensive *Properties* panel is obtained by clicking File — Properties from the *Printers* display. This panel covers both text and graphics printing, and its tabs are described below.

- The Properties panel can vary considerably from one printer type to another, so that the Properties for an inkjet printer are very different from the properties for a laser printer. The illustration shows the second tab of Printer Properties for an inkjet model.

The *General* tab shows the printer name, and has a space for any comment (such as the expected life of a toner or ink cartridge). You can also opt for a separator page with options of *None*, *Full* or *Simple*. The separator is a page that will be printed between documents and is useful if your printer is being used over a network or if you often print documents one after another. A *Full* separator page contains graphics and a *Simple* separator contains text only. You can also prepare a page for yourself (using WMF graphics images along with text), save it, and use the *Browse* button to establish it as a *Separator*.

The *Details* tab contains a large amount of controls that you normally need to set up only once (and you may not need to alter settings). *Print to the following Port* is usually set for port LPT1, and you can click the arrowhead if your printer is connected to another port (including FILE: or a serial port). There are buttons for *Add Port* and *Delete Port* (used mainly for network ports). The *Print using the following Driver* section should show the name of your default printer, and you can click the arrowhead to change to any other installed printer. There is a button for *New Driver* if you are updating a printer driver.

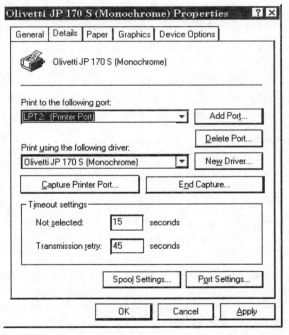

Two more buttons are used for Network printers, labelled *Capture Printer* and *End Capture*. These are used so that you can ensure that you have uninterrupted use of a printer while you print your document, and then release the printer for other users. The *Timeout Settings* are used to avoid error warnings that can appear if the printer is not available. The *Not Selected* time is the time for which Windows will wait for the printer to become available when you start printing a document. You might want to set this to the time it takes for the printer to be ready after switching on. The *Transmission Retry* setting may need to be longer (I use 150 seconds), and it avoids an error message caused by the computer sending data faster than the printer can deal with it. Alter these settings as you need to, based on experience. The other two buttons, at the foot of the panel, are labelled *Spool Settings* and *Port Settings*; these are explained in the *Print Options* for this entry.

• These tabs are common to all printers, but the other tabs differ. For an inkjet printer you are likely to see, typically, tabs labelled *Main*, *Paper* and *Utility*. For a laser printer you may see tabs labelled *Paper*, *Graphics*, *Fonts* and *Device options*.

The *Paper* tab starts with a list of *Paper Sizes*, with the default size (usually A4 in the UK) selected. You can scroll the list sideways to see other acceptable sizes. *Orientation* can be set with option buttons as *Portrait* (default) or *Landscape*. You can set *Paper Source* if you are using a printer with multiple paper trays or cartridges, and also the *Number of Copies*. Click the button marked *Unprintable Area* to see the minimum margins that your printer can use, in units of 0.001 inches or 0.01 mm. These margins are typically about 5 mm for laser printers. If you alter these settings, you can click the *Restore Defaults* button to replace them. The *About* button on the main tab panel will show the printer driver version number, and you can also use the main *Restore Defaults* button to make all settings the default values for your printer.

The *Graphics* tab for a laser printer determines how graphics will be printed, and this tab does not appear for programs that deal with text only. Do not alter these settings until you have had some experience with the graphics programs that you want to use. The *Resolution* setting will show the highest resolution that your printer can produce, and you may want to use a lower value, for example, because you are using ordinary paper with an ink-jet printer, or because you want to match screen resolution, or because your laser printer does not have enough memory for large high-resolution images. *Dithering* settings are provided for colour or grey-scale images, allowing intermediate colours to be produced by alternating dots of different colour, or grey shades to be produced by altering the spacing of black dots. You can opt for *None*, *Fine*, *Coarse*, *Line Art*, or *Error Diffusion*. The general rule is that if you are using resolution of 200 dots per inch or less, select *Fine*, if you are using resolution of 300 dots per inch or more, choose *Coarse* dithering. The *Line Art* setting can be used if all of your work consists of lines only with no colour or grey fillings, and you can opt for *Error Diffusion* if you are printing photographic images with no clear borders.

You may need to experiment with the settings to find what is most appropriate for your own work. The *Intensity* control is set midway by default, and provides the overall value of light or shade for graphics. You can click on the *Restore Defaults* button if you have made alterations and want to get back to normal. Some graphics programs will make the optimum printer settings for you so that you do not need to use these options for yourself.

The *Fonts* tab allows you to select any font *Cartridges* that you are using in a printer. You are unlikely to need this because the use of Windows with TrueType fonts has superseded the need for expensive font cartridges. For printing with TrueType fonts you can use options that are described as *Download as Bitmap Soft Fonts* or *Print TrueType as Graphics*. The *Download* option is the (faster) default and should be used if your document consists mainly of text. If your document contains a large number of graphics and if text is not extensively repeated, the *Graphics* option can be more useful. The *Graphics* option also allows graphics to be printed over text.

The *Device Options* tab applies mainly to laser printers with added memory. You can use this panel to notify the amount of memory in your laser printer and to determine how the memory will be used on a scale from *Conservatively* to *Aggressively*. Use the default settings for memory use unless you are experienced enough to know that you can benefit from altered settings.

• You may see one or more tabs which are labelled with the name of the printer manufacturer. These indicate that the driver has been supplied by the printer manufacturer, and may provide facilities that are not available on drivers supplied from Windows. This is particularly important if the printer has been introduced since your version of Windows became available.

Printing a document: You would normally print a document while you are using the program that created the document, but printing can also be carried out by using Windows 98 methods. For example, you can click with the right-hand mouse button on a document name (in an Explorer view) and then click on *Print*. The document will be opened using the program that created it and printed from that program (for example, a file with the DOC extension will be printed using Word). You can also click the filename with the left-hand mouse button and use the File — Print menu of Explorer, or you can use the *Send To* action of Explorer's *File* menu, with a shortcut to the printer. If you have a printer icon on the Desktop, you can drag the filename to this icon to carry out the print action, or you can keep a shortcut to your printer in the same folder as your document files. These printing options all make use of the program that created the document file and are not intended to be used with a file that already contains printer codes (a file saved using a *Print to File* option). These need to be printed using the MS-DOS command COPY *filename* PRN because this prevents any other program from intervening.

Print status: Printing using Windows 98 is normally *spooled*, meaning that the printing codes produced by the program that is in control will be saved in memory and fed out to the printer as fast as the printer can cope with them. This prevents the computer from being tied up during a print run. You can carry out the *Print* action on a set of documents, which will form a print queue, and these will be dealt with in turn. During this time, a printer icon will appear on the Taskbar and you can double-click this icon or click on it with the right-hand mouse button to get a status report, showing which document is currently printing and what other documents are awaiting printing. You can see this *Status* window also by selecting your printer in the *Control Panel Printers* display, and clicking on File — Open.

• For documents that are not currently being printed, you can alter the order of printing by dragging a file to a different position in the print queue.

• The *Status* window is useful only for files that are being printed either locally or through a network, not for documents that are being printed to a file. If you have not opted for print spooling, no status window will appear.

The *Printer Status* display has a menu set of *Printer*, *Document*, *View*, and *Help*. The *Printer* set contains *Pause*

Windows 98 assistant

Printing, to halt the printer action (local printer only) while you carry out some other task. This is useful if you find that your computer is responding only very slowly while a document is being printed — you can restore action by clicking again to remove the tick. You can also use *Purge Print Jobs* to remove all waiting documents from the print queue (if the printing of a document has started it will be completed). If you are not using your default printer, you can make this setting, and the *Properties* settings, also from the *Printer* menu.

The *Document* menu also contains *Pause Printing* and *Cancel Printing*, and the *View* menu allows you to turn the *Status* bar display of the Window on or off.

Print options: The most important printing option is the use of spooling, and this is set from the Properties — Details tab of the *Printer* item in Control Panel. Click the *Spool Settings* button in this panel to see the *Spooling* panel. The most important option is *Spool print jobs so that program finishes printing faster*, and if you click on the alternative of *Print directly to the Printer*, you will not be able to use the computer while the printer is working.

If you use the default of spooling, you can choose when to start printing, either *After the last page has spooled* or (the default) *After the first page has spooled*. You can select the *Spool Data Format*, which by default is the format called *RAW* Some printers permit the faster *EMF* format to be used. For printers which use a moving printhead, you can enable or disable *Bi-directional Printing*. There is a *Restore Defaults* button at the foot of the panel in case you have lost track of the original settings.

The other button on the *Details* tab of Control Panel — Printers is labelled *Port Settings*. The options in this small sub-panel are to *Spool MS-DOS print jobs* and to *Check*

Port state before printing. These should both normally be checked.

Notes: The Print Screen key, which for MS-DOS programs will print the screen image on paper, acts as a screen capture key in Windows 98, placing the image on the clipboard. You need to use a graphics program to paste the clipboard image in and to print it.

Properties, Web page

General: The *Properties* item can be obtained from the File menu, or by clicking on the document with the right-hand mouse button and then clicking *Properties*. This provides two panels of information about the document, labelled as *General* and *Security*. For some documents only the General tab will appear.

General panel: The *General* panel contains the title of the document, the *Protocol* (typically *File Protocol*), *Type* (usually HMTL) and *URC address* which may be a full Internet address or (for a stored file) a hard drive folder location.

Security panel: This panel will contain security certificate information if you are viewing a secure page.

QuickView

QuickView is a system for viewing documents that were created with some Windows-based programs without starting the program. You can use QuickView only if it has been installed, and if the type of file you want to view is recognised. Note that some very common file types such as PCX are **not automatically** recognised. For some files, QuickView can be used to start an editing action on the file.

Windows 98 assistant

You can also start QuickView by right-clicking on the document and selecting QuickView.

Use: Select a document file that you would like to view , using My Computer or Windows Explorer, and then click File — QuickView. The QuickView will appear in the bar between the folder tree and the file details. If the file cannot be viewed in this way you will see a notice appear, otherwise the QuickView window will open. Most text files can be viewed, along with WMF and BMP graphics files.

Menus and options: The File menu of QuickView contains only *Open File for Editing* and *Exit*. The View menu contains options for *Toolbar*, *Status Bar*, *Page View* and *Replace Window*. For some files, the options for *Landscape* and *Rotate* will be available, and there is also a *Font* option for text files.

Notes: While the QuickView window is open, you can drag another file into it to display.

If you work with each file/folder displayed as a Web page, you will see each selected image file (except PCX types) in quick image form without using QuickView. Other file types such as DOC are displayed, but TXT files are not.

Recycle Bin

General: When you delete a file in the normal way, selecting a name or names and pressing the Delete key or using an Edit — Delete menu, the file is not removed from the disc, and its name and details are simply transferred to another folder labelled as the Recycle Bin. This folder can be accessed from any drive by way of shortcuts. When you empty the Recycle Bin, all of the files contained in the Bin are deleted (though if you have not saved any files subsequently, they may be recoverable by using MS-DOS recovery programs.

Full deletion: If you want to delete a selected file, or set of files, as distinct from using the Bin, press the Shift-Delete keys rather than the Delete key alone. In some circumstances, you will see a message about sending the file to the Recycle Bin, and you will need to click on the *No* button and use Shift-Delete again.

Emptying the bin: There are several methods. If the *Recycle Bin* icon is visible on the Desktop, click on the icon with the right-hand mouse button, and then on *Empty Recycle Bin*. You can also click on the *Recycle Bin* in an Explorer view of *any* hard drive, and then on File — Empty Recycle Bin.

• You can also remove files from the bin selectively, so deleting these files. When you select file(s) and use the Delete key, you will be asked to confirm and reminded that this is a deletion rather than a (reversible) addition to the Recycle Bin.

Restoring files: Files that are contained in the Recycle Bin can be restored. Use the File — Open command for the Bin (either from Desktop or from Explorer). Select one or more files and click File — Restore.

Bin Options: If the Bin icon is visible on the Desktop, click with the right-hand mouse button and then on *Properties*. If you are using Explorer, click on the Bin icon and then on *Properties*. The *Properties* panel will have an additional tab labelled *General* if you start it from the Explorer view of one drive, but this can be ignored. The more important tab is labelled *Global*, followed by tabs for each hard drive or partition of a hard drive.

The Global tab has two option buttons labelled *Configure Drives Independently* (the default) and *Use One Setting for all Drives*. If you opt to use one setting for all drives, the remainder of the panel is available, and you can, if you want, opt not to use the Recycle Bin system at all by clicking on the selection box marked *Do not move files to the Recycle Bin. Remove files immediately when deleted.* You can also opt to declare the maximum percentage of the hard drive(s) that can be used for the Recycle Bin, and you can tick a selection box to *Display delete confirmation dialog*.

- If you use the default option of configuring drives independently, then you can use the tabs that are marked with the letters and names of your hard drives or partitions. Each panel will contain information on the drive size, space reserved for the Recycle Bin files, and the options to delete files directly, not using the Bin, and to declare how much space can be allocated, in that drive, to the Recycle bin.

Note: If disc space is low, opting to delete directly avoids wasting space with unwanted files, but you should ensure that you are using a good backup system. Once you empty the Recycle Bin, all the deleted files are lost unless you have a tape or other backup that includes these files.

Registry

General: The **registry** of Windows 98 is a database that contains a mass of information on the way that Windows and other software operates. This information is contained in two files that should be backed up at intervals. The registry files are checked and (if necessary) altered each time the computer is shut down; this is the reason for the delay between selecting *Shut Down* and getting the message that you can finally switch off.

- Note that the visual Help mentions registry backing up and restoring, but only for networks that use Backup Exec Agent or ARCserve agent software.

Maintenance: Windows 98 uses a utility to check the registry each time the computer is started, creating a backup set of files. If corruption is found, the previous backup will be used, and if no backup is available the utility will try to repair the damage. If the registry contains a reference to a file that has been deleted this will be notified as an error, but removing the reference will prevent the error message from reappearing.

Backup: The registry files are called SYSTEM.DAT and USER.DAT, and are located in the C:\WINDOWS folder. Other backups are stored under different names (not the System.DA0 and User.DA0 used by Windows 95) and new backups are made each time your computer is booted. You should, at intervals, make copies of the DAT files on to a floppy in case of any corruption of the Registry caused by hard drive failure. Though the copies will not be up to date, they will at least contain most of the Registry information that is needed to run the computer as it was configured at the time when the backups were made.

Registry Checker: Registry Checker is a program that reads the Registry contents each time you start your computer. If a problem is found, the backup copy of the Registry is used. This replaces any requirement to perform manual replacement.

You can also run Registry Checker manually by going from the Start button to the System Tools and clicking on *System Information*. In this window, click Tools and then Registry Checker. You can also use this to make another Registry backup.

Windows 98 assistant

Editing: In normal circumstances it should never be necessary to alter the Registry files directly, only by way of options within programs (such as the *File Location* options in Word). You should not on any account alter Registry settings unless advised to do so in a book or a magazine article, and only if you back up the Registry files first. Careless alteration of the Registry files can severely restrict your use of Windows 98.

When it is necessary to edit the registry, you can either use a specialised editor (which will usually allow access only to some specific portions of the Registry) or the REGEDIT utility that is built into Windows 98. To start this editor, click on Start — Run and type REGEDIT (or click the arrowhead to see if this name is already present in the list). The *Editor* panel shows an Explorer-type of display starting with My Computer, and with the six main portions of the Registry displayed with their names, all starting with HKEY. Each main title carries a [+] box that indicates that you can click on the box to expand the display, and most of the HKEY entries will expand to several levels, with information held only in the lowest levels. The database main sections are:

HKEY_CLASSES_ROOT   HKEY_CURRENT_USER

HKEY_LOCAL_MACHINE   HKEY_USERS

HKEY_CURRENT_CONFIG   HKEY_DYN_DATA

Of these, HKEY_CLASSES_ROOT contains information on association of data files with programs, and the sections that you are most likely to use are those that deal with current user, local machine and current configuration.

Registry checker: The System Tools set contains the item System Information, and clicking on this produces another window that contains a Tools menu item. You can click on this and then on the item called Registry Checker to be certain that the Registry is free of errors, and to make another backup if needed.

Notes: From time to time, magazines issue instructions on how to use the Registry for actions that are not available from Windows. You may feel that you are never likely to need these actions, but you should note them because if you ever need to edit the Registry you need all the help you can get.

- The REGEDIT program contains a command that allows you to export the registry files as text. This makes it possible to print the files and examine them at leisure rather than only when REGEDIT is running.

- There is a document called Registry Tips available on the Web site:

http://freespace.virgin.net/alwyn.greenwood/registry.htm

which contains a number of suggestions for modifying the Registry.

Right mouse button

General: The use of the right-hand mouse button was introduced in Windows 95, though some earlier programs featured non-standard actions produced by the right-hand mouse button. In Windows 98 the use of the right-hand mouse button has been extended so that it **always** provides a short menu of useful actions, and the nature of the menu depends on the position of the cursor on the screen at the instant when the right-hand button is pressed. If a program (such as Word or Excel) is running, it may have its own menus for the right-hand button, and the descriptions below refer to its use on the Windows 98 desktop and Taskbar only.

Windows 98 assistant

Taskbar: Clicking with the right-hand button on any unused portion of the Taskbar (**not** on an icon) provides the menu of *Toolbars*, *Cascade*, *Tile Windows Horizontally*, *Tile Windows Vertically*, *Minimize All Windows* and *Properties*. The *Properties* menu item leads to the Taskbar and Start Menu properties panel, see the entries for these items. See also the entry for **cascade/tile** for a description of this action.

Desktop: Clicking with the right-hand button on any unused portion of the Desktop provides the menu of *Active desktop*, *Arrange Icons*, *Line Up Icons*, *Refresh*, *Paste*, *Paste Shortcut*, *Undo Delete*, *New* and *Properties*. The Active Desktop item consists of *View As Web Page* (the default), *Customize my Desktop* and *Update Now*, and if the chosen view is the Web page view, the *Arrange Icon* options are greyed out. These refer to the visible Desktop display if you place several icons on the Desktop.

The *New* item allows the main choice of *Folder* or *Shortcut*, with options for other objects, such as *Word Document*, that depend on what other software you use. The *Properties* item will display the set of tabs for *Display Properties*, see Display.

Recycle Bin: See the **Recycle Bin** entry for the menu that appears when you right-click over this icon.

My Computer: The right-click menu consists of *Explore* or *Open* (sometimes both), *Find*, *Map Network Drive*, *Disconnect Network Drive*, *Create Shortcut*, *Rename* and *Properties*. This provides methods of placing a shortcut to My Computer in another folder, or of renaming it. The *Properties* item leads to the *System Properties* panel that you also find by clicking on *System* in *Control Panel*.

Program name: If you right-click on any of the program names in the Taskbar the menu consists of *Restore*, *Move*, *Size*, *Maximize*, *Minimize*, and *Close*.

Filename: If you right-click on a document filename, the menu consists of *Open*, *Print*, *New*, *Quick View*, *Send To*, *Cut*, *Copy*, *Create Shortcut*, *Delete*, *Rename* and *Properties*.

Notes: You can also drag a file or files using the right-hand mouse button. When you do this, a menu will appear when you drop the file(s) in another folder. The menu is normally *Move Here*, *Copy Here*, *Create Shortcut(s) Here* and *Cancel*, though if you drag to the Recycle Bin you will see only the *Move Here* and *Cancel* options.

Running programs

General: You will normally arrange your favourite programs so that they can be started from the *Start* button menus. This allows starting with a single click even if you have opted for the older double-click method for other items. New programs that you buy will install themselves in this set.

Autostart: Any program that has a shortcut in the Startup folder (C:\Windows\Start) will run automatically when Windows starts. This allows you to have your favourite programs running when Windows starts. Use the Settings — Taskbar and Start Menu option to place program shortcuts into this folder, or drag them into the folder using Explorer. Windows 98 will in the course of use of the Maintenance Wizard rearrange the hard drive so that the programs in the Startup set are loaded more quickly.

Run command: The *Run* command from the *Start* button also offers a way of running programs. This is normally reserved for *Install* programs run from the floppy or CD-ROM drives, and for the **regedit** program used for changing the registry.

Windows 98 assistant

Programs menu: Use the Settings — Taskbar and Start Menu to place programs into any group or to create a new group. You will be guided by a Wizard.

Downloading: If you want to add programs from Internet sites, you should take considerable care to use only sites that can be trusted. See the item on **Security** about *Site Certificates*. Short programs should be downloaded to a floppy. Long programs are likely to be from Microsoft or other known source. You are in danger only if a program from an unknown source is run, but some programs will download and then run automatically. If you download to a floppy or other removable drive you are in less risk.

ScanDisk

General: ScanDisk is a utility that will check the state of discs, hard or floppy, and report on their condition. ScanDisk can also ensure that any faulty areas of a hard drive are locked out of use so that they cannot result in loss of data. ScanDisk is automatically called up by other disc maintenance programs, notably the *Disk Defragmenter*.

Starting: Click Start — Programs — Accessories — System Tools — ScanDisk. The panel that appears asks you to select the drive you want to check. You can opt for either the *Standard check* (files and folders) or the *Thorough check* (files and folders, disc surface). A selection box can be ticked if you want to opt for *Automatically Fix Errors*.

Options: If you use the *Thorough check*, you can click the *Options* button to determine how ScanDisk will deal with your disc. The first options concern the areas of the disc that are scanned, with the options of *System and Data areas* (default), *System area only* and *Data Area only*. There is a selection box that can be ticked for *Do Not Perform Write Testing* and one labelled *Do not Repair Bad Sectors in Hidden and System files*.

Normally, the disc surface is tested by reading the contents of each sector and writing them back to check that the write action does not cause errors. If this box is ticked, only the reading action will be checked — for all but a few exceptional cases you can leave this box un-ticked. The other box concerns the use of programs that expect to find a hidden file in a specific place and which refuse to run unless this file is found. Repairing a bad sector could result in shifting such a file, so that this provision is made for the (now unusual) case of programs that employ this action.

Advanced: The *Advanced* button can be clicked to reveal another set of options on a panel. The set headed *Display Summary* deals with the screen message that appears following ScanDisk, and you can opt for *Always*, *Never* or *Only on Error*. The *Lost File Fragments* section deals with parts of files that have no identification (usually deleted file fragments) and you can opt to *Free* them (so that the space is used by other files) or to *Convert to File* so that you can recover the data, if any. The conversion to a file option is a desperate way of trawling out the remnants of document files that have been deleted from the Recycle Bin.

The *Log File* section deals with the log file of text that reports the ScanDisk results. You can opt for *Replace Log* (old log is replaced by new version), *Append Log* (latest report is added to the end of the previous one) or *No Log*. The *Check Files For* section has selection boxes for *Invalid File Name* and for *Invalid Date/Time*, and you can check both. There is also a selection box that can be ticked for *Check Host Drive First*. This applies to a drive that uses DriveSpace, forcing ScanDisk to check the physical (host) drive before checking the compressed file. This box is ticked by default, and now that DriveSpace is no longer required you can ignore this box. The log file is called SCANDISK.LOG, and is a simple text (ASCII) file located in the C:\ root folder.

Notes: A thorough check on a hard drive can take some considerable time. You will be reminded when you use the My Computer or Explorer *Properties* panel with a hard drive selected, of how many days have elapsed since you carried out a check of your hard drive. You will also be reminded about backups and defragmentation.

Note that you can make the use of ScanDisk a scheduled item.

Scheduled tasks

General: You can use the Maintenance Wizard to carry out the actions of Defragmenter, ScanDisk and Disk Cleanup at scheduled times, and there is also a Task Scheduler that can run any program that you want to schedule. The Task Scheduler runs in the background and leaves a book and clock icon on the Taskbar, usually the first icon on the set at the right hand side of the taskbar.

Opening: Double-click the Task Scheduler icon or click My Computer and then Scheduled Tasks. If you have not used Task Scheduler before there will be only two items appearing, *Add Scheduled Task* and *Tune-up Application Start*. When you have added tasks to the schedule, these will also appear in this display. Tasks can be removed by right-clicking and using the *Delete* item on the menu that appears.

Add tasks: Click the *Add Scheduled Task* item so that the Wizard page appears. Click the *Next* button on the opening page, and you will see a list of programs, corresponding to those that are installed in the Start button menus. You can use a *Browse* button to search for other programs that do not appear in the main list. Click a program to select it, and then click the *Next* button of the Wizard.

You will now see a time schedule page, and you can pick the frequency of use from the list of *Daily*, *Weekly*, *Monthly*, *One time only*, *When my computer starts* and *When I log on*. There is no default here, so that you must make a choice. Click the Next button to see the options for Start time, and frequency — for example, if you have clicked *Weekly* you will see a box marked *Every (1) weeks*, and you can alter the number. Another option for weekly use is the day of the week. If you opted for *Daily*, the choices are *Every Day*, *Weekdays* or *Every (number) days*, with a *Start date*. For monthly use, you can choose a *Day number*, or specify the *first* (second, etc.) *Monday* (or Tuesday, etc.) of the month, and you can also specify which months to use.

When you have scheduled your task in this way, the last page of the Wizard shows a summary, and there is a check box to tick marked *Open advanced properties for this task when I click Finish*. Click the *Finish* button, and if the check box was selected you will see a three-tab display for the program, consisting of *Task*, *Schedule* and *Settings*. The first two tabs summarise what you have scheduled, and provide a way of changing the scheduling. The *Settings* tab provides for other actions with panels for *Scheduled Task Completed*, *Idle Time*, and *Power Management*.

The first of these has a check box for *Delete the scheduled task when finished*, and this should be checked if the task is to be run once only, otherwise left clear. There is also an option for stopping the scheduled task if it is still running after a long time. The default time is 72 hours, but you can alter this figure to whatever suits your needs.

Windows 98 assistant

The *Idle Time* provides for running a scheduled task only if the computer is not being used (no keystrokes or mouse movements), and you can specify how many minutes of idleness to wait before starting the task, and how long to wait to try again if the computer is busy. There is another check box marked *Stop the scheduled task if computer is in use*.

The *Power Management* section deals with the problems of portable machines, and the two check boxes, both ticked by default, are labelled *Don't start scheduled task if computer is running on batteries*, and *Stop the scheduled task if battery mode begins*.

Note: Once a task has been scheduled it will appear on the list and can be edited or deleted as you please.

Scraps

General: A **scrap** is a portion of text or graphics copied from a program to the Desktop. Such a scrap can be dragged into any other suitable document or into a program for editing. This avoids the need to save a selection to a file to be subsequently loaded or inserted into a document or program.

Creating: Make sure that you are working with a portion of the Desktop visible. Select a portion of text or graphics in a program or document. Drag this scrap to the Desktop – it will appear as an icon, and the action is one of copying rather than moving. The icon will carry a name such as *Document Scrap*, along with an identifier such as the first few words of the scrap.

Using: The scrap can be dragged into any *compatible* document or program that supports this action. This does not necessarily mean that you can make use of the scrap. For example, if you create a scrap from a Word document and drag it into Notepad, you will not make much sense of the result. The scrap in this example has to be dragged into a Word (or WordPad) document to be readable. You cannot drag a scrap *from* Notepad.

Notes: Some programs, particularly graphics programs, do not allow scraps to be made, so that the dragging action will not move the selected object out of the Window area. If you hold down the *Shift* key as you drag a scrap to the Desktop, the action will be a *Move* action, so that the scrap disappears from the original document.

The Scraps system is not so useful if you take the option of using a Web-style Desktop with no icons visible.

Script files

General: Script files are a form of programming used along with Dial-Up Networking so that connection to the Internet can be automated. You are not expected to create such files for yourself, and any script files that you might need would normally be provided along with the software you receive from an Internet Provider. The topic of creating and using Script files, in common with all other forms of programming, is beyond the scope of this book.

Security and ratings

General: The Internet developed as a set of files with open access, and enforcing security has been a difficult task. There are several aspects to security. One, the most difficult of all, is to prevent inappropriate material, such as pages promoting crime or perversity, from appearing on your computer, particularly if children use your computer. Another is to ensure that confidential information about you or provided by you cannot be transmitted to anyone who is not entitled to it. A third factor is the use of credit cards to pay for goods or services purchased over the Internet.

Some restriction of viewing can be carried out by using the contents rating system. Some sites contain access to external systems (such as NetNanny) that will prevent inappropriate material reaching your computer except by using your own password. Confidential information and the downloading of programs (guaranteed free of viruses) is carried out using certificates. E-mail security is ensured by using digital Ids and encrypted messages. Security for credit card transactions is provided from the Microsoft Wallet section if this is installed. In addition, Banks and Building Societies now use their own systems to ensure confidentiality and security for money transactions.

Internet ratings: Ratings provide, in theory, a method of restricting access so as to make it difficult for any user to gain access to inappropriate material. The rating system requires the setting up of a password which must be supplied if the ratings are to be altered. The use of ratings does not really solve the problem of offensive material unless you use the option to make un-rated pages inaccessible, see later. Offensive sites are unlikely to apply for a rating, and you are likely to see offensive language turning up in the course of a search even for technical terms. If you use News, there is little chance of avoiding offensive material, because News, particularly in the *alt* sections, is widely used specifically for such purposes. Worse still, some of these sites may obtain your email address and send offers to you. Even Search actions can turn up such material because words that you are searching for appear in an offensive Web site.

Creating rating password: With Internet Explorer running, click View — Internet Options — Content and click *Enable*.

Enter your password — you are asked to enter the same password twice as a confirmation. Once this has been done, you can click the *Settings* button (and provide the password) to view the ratings. You should take a **secure** note of your password if you want to be able to alter ratings again at any time. If you forget your password you will find it very difficult to alter or switch off your ratings (you cannot find your password again, and you will have to alter registry settings to reset the system to where it was before a password was imposed).

Creating ratings: Click a category for each item in the list which consists of *Language, Nudity, Sex* and *Violence*. For each category, you can use a slider control to set the level which you consider acceptable, from *None* to *Extreme levels*. If you are online at the time, you can click a button to see the Internet page for the source of ratings advice. Note that there are no ratings specifically for racial or religious offensiveness.

Enforcing ratings: Click on the *General* tab of the *Ratings* page. There are two user options here. If you leave the first unticked, *Users can see sites which have no rating*, you ensure that a site which has not been rated cannot be viewed. If you tick this box, a user may see material on a site that has not been rated and which might therefore contain very offensive material. On the other hand you might be prohibiting access to a completely innocuous site, such as flight arrivals, which is simply not subject to ratings. The other options box allows a user with a password to obtain access to rated material which you have restricted. Tick this box to ensure that you alone can gain access to such material, or use a password as you wish. Remember again that forgetting a password will lock you out of making changes. If you leave the box blank the pages cannot be viewed.

Windows 98 assistant

Advanced ratings: The *Advanced* section of the *Ratings* panel allows you to change to another ratings system if one is available. The default is the RSACi system, and no other is currently named in the list, so that this action is available only to cope with later developments. Note that Web sites outside the USA will often ignore these US-based ratings systems.

Certificates: Certificates can be personal or site based. A personal certificate is based on your name and password and is used so that you can identify yourself when you send information out. A Web site certificate assures you that a site uses a security system that makes it safe to use, whether for sending confidential information or for downloading programs that can be used without fear of virus or other problems. You cannot initiate certificates for yourself, only in conjunction with a secure site. Turn to View — Internet Options — Content and look at the *Certificates* section.

Examine certificates: No *Personal* certificates will be available unless you have created one with the co-operation of a secure site. When you examine the *Sites list*, you will see a list of sites, all in USA or Canada:

The *Publishers* list pertains to software, and will normally be empty unless you have entered information from a software publisher. You can tick the box to accredit as trustworthy all commercial software publishers. You can inspect the dates for site certification agencies by clicking on the name and then on *View Certificate* button. Click on the *Expiration Date* to see the date, usually 31/12/1999, for the certification.

Warnings: If a site is not secure, you can be warned. Click on View — Internet Options — Advanced to see options for turning on warnings of changing between secure and insecure sites, of invalid site certificates, and of accepting cookies (files that identify you to Web sites).

Transactions security: Click View — Internet Options — Advanced and look at the Security settings. The default is to accept all levels of security, named PCT1, SSL2, and SSL3 . If you opt only for PCT or SSL3 you may be unable to use some sites, but SSL2 is usable by all secure sites. An option is to click the box marked *Do not save secure pages to disk*, which prevents confidential material appearing on your hard drive (which may not be secure). If you use Net banking, this option is applied whether you have clicked it or not.

Money transactions: *Personal Information* is the last section of the Content page. This consists of a set of buttons marked *Edit Profile*, *Reset Sharing*, *Addresses* and *Payments*. The *Edit Profile* button leads to a set of six tabs of which you can probably make use of only the first three, calling for your name, *E-mail*, *home address* and *business address*. You need not fill these in if you do not want to, and Explorer will warn you if any site wants to read the information. The last tab *Digital Ids*, establishes another layer of security for e-mail messages, but will only be useful if the scheme is being operated by one of your contacts.

* Omitting your e-mail in the *Personal Information* section is a good defence against junk e-mail.

The *Microsoft Wallet* section allows you to load in addresses from your Address book, or to type in the information for addresses that will be involved in making credit card payments. The *Payments* section selects the types of credit cards you will be using and allow entry providing that a contact address exists. Note that this section allows the entry of credit card details for Visa, Mastercard and American Express only at present.

Downloaded programs: see under **active content** for security of downloaded programs.

Selecting

General: You can select a folder or filename so that you can carry out an action, such as copying or deleting, on that file or folder. More important, you can select more than one file or folder as a group so that an action such as copying or deleting will apply to all in the group.

Default: The default for Windows 98 Explorer is that a file or folder is selected when the pointer is over it. Clicking on the name (which is underlined) will **open** the file or folder. You can hold down the Ctrl key and place the pointer on another name to add this to the selection (or you can point again to deselect one name). You can use the Edit — Select All menu item to select all the files in one folder. You can select one file, hold down the Shift key and then point to another file to select all the files (inclusively) that lie between the two you have clicked.

• You can also drag a selection window around a set of files (press the left-hand mouse button near one file and drag to another). On a Web page view this is easier to do if you start dragging from the right-hand side — you may find it impossible to drag from the left in a Web view page.

Options: You can opt to use the older Windows 95 system in which you click over a file to select it, and double-click to run the file. To make this option, run Windows Explorer and use View — Folder options. In the *General* tab, click *Classic style* and then the *OK* button. If you want to use the Web page style, but with other options, click *Custom* and then the *Settings* button. This brings up the various options relating to Active desktop, browsing folders, viewing Web content, clicking and underlining.

MS-DOS text selection: If you have opened a document using an MS-DOS program, you may not be able to use mouse selection. If you cannot use the mouse to drag over text, click Edit — Mark and then click at the start of the text you want to select. Hold down the Shift key, and click on the end of the text block. You can then use the Edit — Copy menu action to put the text on the Clipboard, from which it can be pasted into any other program that is editing a document, MS-DOS or Windows.

Notes: See the **MS-DOS** entry for the actions of *Quick Edit* and *Fast Paste* applied to documents opened under MS-DOS.

Sending

General: The *Send To* action is a file action that is available from My Computer or Explorer, or from the right-hand mouse button menu when a filename is selected. The default destination for the *Send To* action is a floppy drive, but you can add other destinations in a folder called *Send To*.

Using: Select the file you want to use, click with the right-hand mouse button, and then on the *Sent To* item. Click on the destination that you want to use.

Destination: Using My Computer or Explorer, click on the C:\WINDOWS\Send To folder. Use the File — New menu item and select *Shortcut*. You will see the Shortcut Wizard appear and you can type a destination or click the *Browse* button to find a suitable destination

Notes: Remember that when you use a shortcut to a printer, this will start up a suitable program when you use *Send To*. For example, if you use *Send To* (aimed at the printer) on a DOC file, Word will be started, the document loaded in, and the *Print* action of Word used.

Shortcuts

General: A shortcut is a small file, usually about 128 bytes, which is a form of path-pointer to a program or document file or to a device such as a floppy disc drive or printer. The advantage of using shortcuts is that they can be placed in any folder, avoiding the need to have to remember a path to a destination. More than one shortcut can be used referring to one destination. A shortcut icon can be identified by the small curly arrow at the bottom left-hand corner.

Creating: By far the simplest method is to use the Wizard, starting from an Explorer or My Computer display. Click on the folder in which you want to place the shortcut. Click File — New and then *Shortcut*. Either type the name of the object or folder, or use *Browse* to find the object or folder, and click for the next step of the Wizard. Another method that is particularly useful for a file is to click on the name, hold down the Ctrl and Shift keys, then drag the filename to the destination folder where you want the shortcut established.

Deleting: Select the shortcut and press the Delete key. Deleting a shortcut does not delete the object or program to which it is a shortcut.

Copying: Use an Explorer or My Computer view, click the shortcut, and then Edit — Copy. Open the folder that is to receive the Shortcut and click Edit — Paste.

Settings: Click the shortcut using the right-hand mouse button, and then click the *Properties* item on the menu. The *General* panel that appears contains information about the Shortcut file, and clicking the *Shortcut* tab will show information that is more useful to you, particularly the *Target*, *Start In*, *Shortcut keys*, and *Run* lines. The *Target* line shows the path to the file or object that the shortcut leads to, and the *Start In* line will often show the same folder, but can show a folder that is used to start a program. The *Shortcut key* (or hot key) line will by default show *None*, but you can click in this line and then press down keys that you will use to start the shortcut. You must include the Ctrl or Alt key (or both) and a letter key. Because the shortcut key line will not accept key combinations that are used in Windows you may find that the combination is not exactly as you typed (you might press Ctrl-N and get Ctrl-Alt-N).

Note: Do not make more shortcuts than you need. Although a shortcut file is short (128 bytes), each one will take up at least a 4 Kbyte cluster on the hard drive.

Shut down programs

General: When you install Windows 98 you are asked to shut down all running programs with the exception of Explorer and Systray. For other installation actions also it can be useful to shut down programs, and the same method is used to deal with a program that has for some reason ceased to respond to keys or mouse movement and seems to be jammed.

Action: Press the Ctrl, Alt and Del keys simultaneously (the Ctrl–Alt–Del action). You will see a list of running programs, including some that are being used by Windows (such as Systray) that you may not be aware of. Select a program name and then use the End Task button to close the program. You can shut down your computer by clicking on the Close Program button or by using Ctrl–Alt–Del keys again.

Sound Recorder

General: The Sound Recorder can be used if you have a sound card and a suitable microphone, CD player, tape cassette player, or other sound source, plugged into it. You can then create sound 'objects' represented by icons for WAV files that can be pasted into documents. Clicking on a sound object icon will play the sound. You need some knowledge of digital sound recording principles to get the best out of Sound Recorder. You will probably need a considerable amount of trial and error to obtain satisfactory results, particularly with a microphone.

Starting: Click Start — Programs — Accessories — Multimedia — Sound Recorder, or click the file SNDREC32.EXE in an Explorer display. You can place a shortcut to this file in any folder or on the Desktop if you want faster access.

Creating a sound object: Make sure that your microphone, preferably a good moving-coil type, is plugged into the sound card. Start *Sound Recorder* and click the File — New item. The icons at the bottom of the pane represent the usual cassette recorder symbols for Play, Record, Stop, Fast forward and Fast back. Click the *Record* icon (round dot) to begin recording and the *Stop* icon (rectangle) when you have finished. Use File — Save As to save the sound as a file. Remember that a fairly short speech can require a fairly large amount of memory space unless you opt for telephone-quality. If you use a CD player or cassette-player as your sound source you will need to opt for higher quality and use much more disc space.

Playing a sound: You can replay a sound using either *Sound Recorder* or *Media Player* (see entry). To replay from *Sound Recorder*, click File — Open and click the name of a sound file you have recorded. Click the *Play* button to start, and the *Stop* button to stop. You can also use the 'fast wind' controls to move to the start or the end of a sound recording.

Audio Properties: Click the *Sound Recorder* Edit — Audio Properties menu item to see the panel which is in two parts, *Playback* and *Recording*, and for each there is a slider volume control. The preferred device that appears for each will be the sound card that is installed on your computer. You should ensure that the box marked *Show Volume Control on the Taskbar* is ticked – see the entry for **Volume Control.**

Options: With the *Audio Properties* panel displayed, click *Advanced Properties*. The panel that appears for Playback allows you to select your speaker setup and has a *Performance* tab that can be used if you experience problems such as broken sound or poor quality. Use the default settings unless you experience problems or know what the effects of changes will be. Using the *Best* setting of *Sample rate* will result in very large files. You can use the *Restore Defaults* button if you have made too many changes. For recording, only the *Performance* tab is used in the *Advanced* section, and the same remarks apply.

Sound in a document: You can insert or link a sound file into a document, such as a text file in Word. Open the sound file using *Sound Recorder*, and click Edit — Copy. Now open the document and click the place in the document where you want the sound icon to be put. Click Edit — Paste. If you want to link the sound file, use the Edit — Paste Special option and select *Paste Link*. If there is no *Paste Special* option in the *File* menu, the program that holds the document does not support linking and only embedding can be used. An embedded sound can make a document length very much greater than you would expect from the amount of text that it contains.

Windows 98 assistant

Recording/Playback Formats: When you click File —
Properties you will see the *Details* tab that shows the Audio
format and other details of a sound file. The default format is
labelled as PCM 22,050 Hz, 8 Bit, Mono. You can click the
Convert Now button to open another panel open with
displays for *Name*, *Format* and *Attributes*, and buttons
marked *Save As* and *Remove*. The range of name (click the
arrowhead) is *Untitled*, *CD quality*, *Radio quality* and
Telephone quality. This form of naming makes it easier to
select the quality level that you need, and you can read the
Attributes panel to see what *Format* and combination of
Attributes are used. If you alter the *Format* or the *Attributes*,
the name will change to *Untitled*, allowing you to create a
quality level for your own use. The fixed names are:

Telephone quality	11K	8-bit mono	11 KB/s
Radio quality	22K	8-bit mono	22 KB/s
CD quality	44K	16-bit stereo	172 KB/s

with the figures showing, in order, the sampling rate,
number of bits per sample, and number of kilobytes per
second. The sampling rate is the number of samples of the
sound wave per second used to convert the wave into a set of
numbers for digital recording.

- Unless you have some experience with audio equipment
  you cannot be expected to make head or tail of the
  details, and the quality names are a more useful guide.
  Remember that higher quality means larger files.

If you want to make a scheme of your own you can choose
from the formats and attributes that are on offer – these may
depend on which sound card you are using. A typical list is
CCITT A-Law, *CCITT µ-Law*, *Creative ADPCM*, *Creative
FastSpeech 10*, *Creating FastSpeech 8*, *DSP Group
TrueSpeech*, *GSM 6.10*, *IMA ADPCM*, *Microsoft ADPCM*,

MSN Audio and *PCM* (the usual default). Your own scheme can be named and saved using the *Save As* button.

Editing sounds: When you have made a sound recording, you can edit it as if it were on a tape. You can delete a part of the sound file by moving the *Recorder* position indicator (slider) to the point where you want to start cutting. Now click Edit — Delete After Current Position to delete all that follows, or Edit — Delete Before Current Position to delete all that comes earlier in the file.

If the *Sound Recorder* display shows a green line (to indicate that the file uses an uncompressed format) you can change the playback speed by using Effects — Increase Speed or Effects — Decrease Speed. Each change is up by 100% (doubled) or down by 50% (halved). The volume of an uncompressed file can also be changed in 25% increments by using the *Effects* menu. Uncompressed files can also be played in reverse using Effects — Reverse and then clicking the *Play* button, and an echo can be added using Effects — Add Echo.

- Any changes that you have made to a sound file which has not been saved can be cancelled by using File — Revert. Once you save a file the changes are fixed.

You can use the *Edit* menu items of *Insert File* and *Mix with File* (which also exist in *Paste* versions) to replace part of an existing sound file with another sound file (*Insert*) or to mix the files so that you hear the sound of both. This is easier if you have had some experience of conventional sound mixing, and the actions are possible only if the sound files are uncompressed.

Notes: If you need to keep a document size down, you can link in the sound objects. Making an ASCII version of a document will cut out all sound objects.

Sound, Web

General: Sound is available over the Internet provided that you have a sound card, loudspeakers and suitable software installed. Sound files are enabled by default, but can be disabled to allow faster downloading.

Suppression: Click View — Internet Options — Advanced and turn off the *Play sounds* option in the Multimedia section.

Start button

General: The *Start* button is the starting point for most of the Windows 98 actions. Many of these actions have already been described under other headings, so that most of the following is a summary only of the *Start* button actions.

Run: The *Run* item is used when you need to run a program that is not normally available. It can be used for REGEDIT (see the entry for **Registry**), for example, and for running setup programs from a floppy. The arrowhead on the *Run* line can be clicked to select commands that have been used in the past. You should not use *Run* unless you are directed to, because installing modern programs should be done by using the Control Panel *Add/Remove Programs* item.

- Run can, however, be used to open shared folders over a network.

Help: The Help item will start the main Windows 98 Help system, allowing you to look up help topics in the index, or to search for help.

Find: The Find item will start the *Find* action which is available also from Explorer.

Settings: This item brings up a sub-menu of *Control Panel*, *Printers* and *Taskbar*. These settings can be made also from Explorer. Remember that if Explorer (or the Explorer window of My Computer) is running when you shut down the computer, it will automatically start again when you switch on.

Documents: This menu item will reveal all the most-recently edited document names, in the form of shortcuts placed in a *Documents* folder. You can load a document into the program that created it, and edit the document, by clicking on the document name in this list. You can use Start — Settings — Taskbar to see a *Clear* button which can be clicked to remove all *Document* shortcuts. You should clear out the *Document* list at intervals, because a large number of shortcuts can take up a disproportionate amount of space on your hard drive.

Programs: This item leads to the main folder list, starting with *Accessories* and containing *MS-DOS Prompt* and *Windows Explorer*. You can add other sets using Explorer.

Adding/removing programs: When Windows 98 was installed on your computer, a set of programs was placed into the *Start* menu, and programs that you have installed since will also have been added. You may want to place other programs into the Start set, however. The simplest method is to open the *Start Menu* folder of C:\WINDOWS and open whichever subfolder you want to use (such as *Programs*, *Accessories*, etc.). You can then create a shortcut to the program you want in that subfolder. You can remove programs from the *Start* menu by deleting the corresponding shortcut in its subfolder.

The more formal method is to click Start — Settings — Taskbar and click the *Start Menu Programs* tab. You can opt to *Add* or *Remove* a program, and a Wizard will then guide you through the process. When you opt to *Add*, you can click a *Browse* button to assist you in finding the path to the program you want. The *Advanced* button of this set simply leads to an Explorer type of display so that you can work with the folders directly rather than through the Wizard.

- Any program file shortcuts that you place into the *Startup* subfolder will run when you start Windows, so that you can have all of your favourite programs running when you start. You can click the shortcut name with the right-hand mouse button and click the *Properties* item to determine whether you want to be able to use a shortcut key combination, or what size of window to use when the program is started.

- You can add new sub-folders to the *Start* Menu set by using Explorer and creating a new folder in the usual way.

- You do not need to put Explorer in the Startup menu – it will restart automatically if it was running when you shut down Windows 98.

Log Off (name): This option allows you to end your Windows session so that another user can take over. The other user may run Windows with entirely different settings, and will always open Windows with these settings. When you use Windows again, the settings will be those that you have specified. When you log off, the Windows desktop will appear with a panel for User name and Password, so that each user can be identified. Do not use a password unless you need to. Click the OK button to start Windows again.

Shut Down: You use this option to shut down the computer in an orderly way, so that the **Registry** (see entry) can be modified to accommodate any changes that you have made. You should not simply switch off. Click the *Shut Down* option and select which option you want, usually *Shut Down* (options of *Restart* and *Restart in MS-DOS Mode*). You can use the *No* button if you change your mind at this point. While the Registry is being updated you will see a screen message asking you to wait, and you should not switch off until you see a message in red telling you that it is now safe to do so. If you switch off prematurely you risk losing data.

A *Standby* item will appear in this set if your computer is a modern type with power-saving options. In Standby mode, the computer consumes very little power but is ready to restart much more quickly than it would if it had been switched off.

Notes: The Start menu operates by using shortcuts, see the entry for **Shortcuts**.

Startup files and folder

General: The *Startup* folder contains shortcuts to programs, and when Windows 98 is started, these programs will be loaded and run. You can determine for each program whether it will run full-screen, in its default window size, or minimised. This allows you to start Windows with all your favourite programs ready to use. Note that you do not need to have Explorer (or the Explorer format of My Computer) in this set because these programs will start automatically if they have been in use when the computer was closed down.

You can also use Windows Explorer to create new folders (using File — New) in any part of the Start Menu. You can, for example, click the *Programs* folder and create new folders called *Communications*, *Data*, *Drawing*, *Financial*, etc., so that your *Programs* list contains these new titles, and you can then place program shortcuts into these folders.

Add/Remove programs: By far the simplest way, when you have some experience with Explorer, is to display the

C:\WINDOWS\Start Menu\Programs\Startup folder. You can then create shortcuts in this folder for the programs you want, and you can also delete shortcuts to programs that you no longer need to be loaded ready for you.

The other method is to use Start — Settings — Taskbar, and click the *Start Menu Programs* button. You can opt to *Add* or *Remove* programs and the Wizard will then guide you to browse for the program you want to add or find the program you want to remove. The *Advanced* button can be clicked to allow you to use Explorer to alter files and folders and read the Properties of files and shortcuts to files.

Notes: You do not need to place Explorer or My Computer in the Startup menu. If either or both of these programs is running when you switch off it will resume when you re-start the computer.

If you had placed program shortcuts in the *Startup* menu, and you subsequently move the programs, you must delete the shortcuts and make new ones. If you forget to do this you may find that the system hangs or the action is simply ignored.

Status bar

General: The status bar of a Windows 98 program is located at the bottom of the window, and carries information on your current folder or file selection. For example the status bar of Explorer shows the size of a selected file, the size of a selected folder, and the free space on a selected hard drive or floppy disc.

Switching: You can usually switch the status bar display on or off. For example, when you are using Explorer, you can click View — Status Bar to switch the bar on (tick appears in menu) or off.

Notes: The information that appears in a Status Bar is often useful, so that you should preferably opt to make this item visible.

System

General: The system files of Windows 98 and MS-DOS are programs that are essential to the running of the operating system. System files **must not** be deleted, and in some cases should not even be moved, so that Windows 98 allows the names of system files to be concealed in an Explorer display.

Concealing: From Explorer, click View — Folder options to see the *View* tab. Look at the *Hidden Files* section. The default setting is *Show All Files*, but you can alter this by clicking either *Do not show hidden or system files* or *Do not show hidden files.*

Notes: The majority of system files are **DLL** (dynamic link library) types, and your system may not use some of them. You can use the File — Properties item of Explorer to find out what the file is used for, selecting the *Version* tab, and clicking *Product Name*. If the *Product Name* is Windows 98, it is fairly certain that you might cause problems by deleting such a file. If the *Product Name* shows a program that you have deleted or which you have not installed, you might be able to delete the file.

Many DLL files are shared, however, so that you cannot be certain whether a file is used or not. If you delete a DLL file, keep it on the Recycle Bin or on a floppy until you are quite certain you don't need it. Some files may be used only at infrequent intervals so that you would not know that you had deleted an important DLL file until you tried to use a program that required it.

Windows 98 assistant

System file checker: Windows 98 incorporates the System File Checker (SFC) for restoring system files that have been damaged (usually by badly behaved applications). The file checker will display a notice and you can opt to update the information (if a new file has been installed and is known to be acceptable), restore the old file, or ignore the warnings. A log of changes is created and is named SFCLog.txt. The System File Checker can also extract files from your Windows 98 CD-ROM

You can start the Checker by moving to the System Tools section of the Start menu and clicking *System Information*. When this opens, click its Tools menu and then *System File Checker*. The panel that appears has two options, *Scan for altered files* (the default), and *Extract one file from installation disk*. The *Settings* button can be clicked to find options on backing up files, making a log and checking for changed or deleted files. A *Search Criteria* tab allows you to determine which folders to check and whether to check subfolders. If a corrupted or altered file is found you will see a panel appear with options for restoring the file or marking the new version as acceptable. You can also select file types. The default settings should be left as they are until you have some experience of using the Checker (which you might never need). An *Advanced* tab provides for using different data files or restoring the data file that existed when Windows 98 was installed.

System information: Is used to provide a summary of your system for the benefit of anyone looking for ways of solving a problem — you are not expected to make use of the information unless you have technical knowledge. The point is that you can save the information to send to a supplier of hardware or software if problems arise. You can start the System Information panel from the System Tools folder in the Start menu.

Tape drives

General: The use of tape drives for Backup is much better supported in Windows 98 than in Windows 95, including the types of drive that use the IDE connection (the same as is used for the hard drive). For use of tape drives, see the entry for Backup.

Taskbar

General: The Windows 98 Taskbar is the strip at the foot of the screen which displays the *Start* button along with buttons for any programs that are running. The right-hand corner of the Taskbar can also display icons, such as the loudspeaker (for *Volume Control*), other programs, and the time. The Web options of Explorer, Outlook Express, Channels and Show Desktop are also on the Taskbar. The Taskbar can be hidden so that it appears only when needed (when the pointer is moved to the foot of the screen).

Position: The Taskbar can be dragged to the top or either side of the screen. When it is dragged to the side, most of the titles will be cut short, but you can place the cursor on the edge of the bar, so that the double-arrow cursor appears, and then drag out the width of the Taskbar. For most purposes, the default position is better.

Options: Click Start — Settings — Taskbar & Start Menu. The four selection boxes on the *Taskbar Options* panel are marked *Always on Top*, *Auto Hide*, *Show Small Icons in Start Menu*, and *Show Clock*. The *Always on Top* item should be ticked, as it ensures that the Taskbar can always be seen over a maximised window. You can use *Auto Hide* if you like to run programs maximised, and do not want to lose part of the window space to the Taskbar. If you use this option, you will see the Taskbar appear only when you move the mouse pointer to the bottom of the screen and hold it there. The *Show Small Icons* option can be clicked if you feel that the icon size in the Start menu looks too large on a 640×480 display – on 800×600 or higher the problem is usually to see icons without using a magnifying glass. Click the *Show Clock* icon for a display of time at the bottom right-hand corner of the Taskbar. Placing the cursor on this time display will bring up a date display.

Programs: When a program name appears on the Taskbar (in minimised form) you can click with the left-hand mouse button to restore the program to the active window, or you can click with the right-hand mouse button to close the program. The Alt-Tab key method of switching from one program to another (as used on Windows 3.1) can be used also on Windows 98, and does not require the Taskbar to be visible.

- You can minimise all open windows by clicking a blank place on the Taskbar using the right-hand mouse button and selecting *Minimize All Windows*. If you then click again on a blank portion of the Taskbar, you will find that the menu includes *Undo Minimize All*, allowing you to restore all windows.

- When the printer is in use with spooling (the default) a printer icon will appear on the right hand side of the default Taskbar. Click this icon to see the print queue display.

Notes: If you keep a large number of programs running, the Taskbar descriptions will be very brief.

Text

General: The text that appears in Windows 98, as distinct from text in editing or word-processing programs, can be copied and changes to fonts can be made. Even the Help screens allow a choice of fonts.

Copying text: Select the text (in a dialogue box or a Help box) that you want to copy and then click on the selected text with the **right-hand** mouse button. As an alternative, you can right-click on the text and on *Select All*. Click the *Copy* commands in the menu. Switch to a text editor or word processor and use the *Paste* action to complete the copying. Text can also be copied from one dialogue box to another, using the *Paste* command (if available) from the right-hand mouse button menu.

Font and size: Start Control Panel from Explorer or from Start — Settings. Click on *Display*, and on the *Appearance* tab. Click *Custom* to change the font size for displays of 800 × 600 or higher. For such displays, you can also opt to make the screen display match actual size. Hold a ruler, calibrated in inches, against the image of a ruler on the panel, and drag the end of the screen ruler so that it exactly matches the size of the real ruler. The drawback of this is that some fonts may then appear much too small for easy reading on a 14 inch screen. Note that these changes do **not** apply if you are using the default 640 × 480 screen resolution.

- See the entry for **Desktop** for changing fonts and sizes of text in standard window displays. See the **Help** entry for changing Help fonts.

Notes: If you make changes to the Desktop appearance, save your Desktop setup as a file so that you can restore it if you subsequently make other changes that you regret.

Toolbar, IE4

General: Internet Explorer makes use of a multi-section toolbar. By default this consists of three sections, but it can be compressed by dragging. See the entry for **icons** for a picture of toolbar icons of Explorer, Mail and News.

Enable/disable: Use View — Toolbar to enable or disable the toolbar sections.

Navigating: The toolbar contains a number of icons for navigation, including *Home, Search* and *Favourites,* and the *Links* toolbar contains icons for useful sites.

Appearance: Use View — Internet Options — Advanced to change two aspects of the toolbar appearance. The Toolbar section contains selection boxes marked *Show Font buttons* and *Small Icons*, and you can tick or untick these.

Tools

General: The main System Tools of Windows 98 are Backup, Disk Defragmenter, Disk Cleanup and ScanDisk. Backup enables you to copy data in compressed form on floppies, tapes, other computers on a network, or removable hard drives. Disk Defragmenter will reorganise your files on the hard drive so that there are no gaps. Disk Cleanup will keep the hard drive from being filled with unwanted files, and ScanDisk will check a hard drive for errors, recover defective file fragments, and ensure that any faulty portions of the drive are not used. See the entries for these specific items.

Other tools: *Compression Agent* is used only on hard drives that have been compressed by using *Drivespace*. You do not need to use this system now that large hard drives are available at low prices.

The *Maintenance Wizard*, *Scheduled Tasks* and *System Information* tools are all useful at intervals, and are dealt with under separate headings in this book.

ToolTips

General: *ToolTips* are the short messages that appear under the mouse pointer when you hold the pointer over an icon. The use of *ToolTips* can be switched on or off in some programs, though not in Windows itself, and the appearance of the tips can be changed.

Appearance: Start Control Panel from Explorer or from Start — Settings and click Display. Select the *Appearance* tab, and click the arrowhead on the *Item* line. Scroll down to the *ToolTips* item. You can then change the colour of background used for *ToolTips*, and the font type, size and colour of the printing in a *ToolTip*.

Notes: If a program allows you to switch *ToolTips* on or off you should preferably work with *ToolTips* on. Some older programs will not permit the use of *ToolTips*.

Troubleshooters

General: Several Help pages in Windows 98 contain Troubleshooters that can be started by clicking. You should follow the guidelines, below, so that you can make effective use of these Troubleshooters.

Preparation: Position the Help page that contains the Troubleshooter so that you can see the text. Close or minimise all windows that are not relevant — it is sometimes quicker to use the *Minimize all Windows* command (right-click in vacant Taskbar space) and then enlarge the Help window. Place the Help screen in the right hand side of the screen and click the *Hide* icon on the Help toolbar so that the index disappears.

Running the Troubleshooter: When you click the Troubleshooter you will see options that allow you to provide information. Once you have provided the information, you can click a Next button for another page, and you will be asked at intervals if what you have done is effective. Follow the instructions precisely.

USB

General: USB is the Universal Serial Bus, a method of connecting all the slower peripherals (such as mouse, keyboard, joystick, modem, and printer) to the computer. This type of bus replaces the older serial type, and runs much faster (12 million bits per second). This rate is adequate for connecting CD-ROM and MPEG-2 video cards, so that the USB can handle sound and images as well as text or program data.

Connection: A computer with USB has a single connection, and this is used with a *hub* that connects to the port and provides, typically, five outlets. Up to 127 devices can be connected by using larger hub units. The aim is to permit practically all the peripherals to be connected through a single port, making it easier to add peripherals.

Equipment: The units that are connected must be to USB standard, so that your existing older equipment will not be useful. All USB attachments will be plug and play, and hot connection (with the computer working) is possible.

Note: At the time of writing, new motherboards were fitted with USB, though the matching peripherals had not yet emerged. Another form of communication, *Firewire*, may eventually be used for faster data, and though it is not a standard fitting on motherboards at the time of writing, it is used on digital camcorders.

Digital audio: Windows 98 supports the use of USB along with digital loudspeakers (initially from Philips and Altec-

Lansing), so that no sound card is needed if these devices are used along with USB.

View menus

General: The View menu is used on both versions of Explorer to configure screen displays and deals with bars, fonts, source-code and options. The *View* options are dealt with separately, following. Windows Explorer contains a View menu with Folder options and Internet Explorer contains a View menu with Internet Options

Toolbars: Can be clicked to choose the display of Toolbars. The Toolbars are named as Standard Buttons, Address Bar, Links and Text Labels, and you can opt to have any combination you want.

Status bar: Can be clicked to turn the status bar display at the foot of the screen on or off. Since the status bar displays useful reminder messages, you should preferably keep it turned on.

Explorer Bar: Allows you to turn off the Explorer bar (the wide bar at the left-hand side of the Explorer screen), or use it for Search, Favorites, History, or Channels. Windows Explorer also uses an *All Folders* option.

Fonts (IE): This appears only in Internet Explorer and allows a choice of five font sizes for Web pages, both on-screen and for printed output. The sizes are given simply as *Largest, Large, Medium, Small* and *Smallest*. Font styles are selected from Options — General, see later.

Stop (IE): This appears only in Internet Explorer and will stop the downloading of a Web page, and can be used if you find that a page is taking an inordinate amount of time (and telephone charges). Shortcut is the Esc key.

Windows 98 assistant

Refresh: Can be used to refresh the information on a Web page or a file display if any part of the display has become corrupted or if information has altered. Shortcut is the F5 key.

Source (IE): This appears only in Internet Explorer and it displays the HTML code that is used to create the current Web page. You can edit this to change the page, and use it to create a page of your own. It is easier, however, to use specialised Web page editor programs. The Edit commands of *Cut, Copy* and *Paste* can be used on the source-code display.

Internet options (IE): This appears only in Internet Explorer and it displays a set of six panels with tab names of *General, Security, Content, Connection, Programs* and *Advanced*. These options are dealt with in detail under the separate heading, following.

Folder options (WE): This appears only in Windows Explorer and uses tabs *General* and *View* to determine how closely Windows Explorer resembles Internet Explorer. A third tab appears when a folder is selected, and contains the options for *File Types*, see the entry for **Association**.

View options, IE

General: The View options allow you to configure your copy of Internet Explorer to work in a way that suits your needs. You should not alter the settings, however, until you have had some experience of using Internet Explorer.

Options: Displays a set of six panes with tab names of *General, Connection, Navigation, Programs, Security* and *Advanced*. These options are dealt with in detail following. The View options allow you to configure your copy of Internet Explorer to work in a way that suits your needs.

You should not alter the settings, however, until you have had some experience of using Internet Explorer.

The *General* pane is divided into sections headed *Home page*, *Temporary Internet Files* and *History*, and with four buttons marked *Colors*, *Fonts*, *Language* and *Accessibility*.

The *Home page* section allows you to set as Home page the current Web page you are viewing, the *Default* for your system, or a blank page. If there is a page you use frequently you can save time by making this your Home page. For some purposes, you might prefer a blank page.

Temporary Internet files are used for storing material you have downloaded, and this section of the *General* pane allows you to delete these files or to specify how these files are treated, using the *Settings* button. The first portion of the Settings page allows you to update files on each visit to a page, every time IE4 is activated, or never. The page visit option is the default. Updating each time Explorer is started can make startup very slow.

The second part of this tab allows you to specify what fraction of the hard drive capacity can be used for these files. A setting of around 5% is reasonable, and using larger amounts allows you to keep more in store. When the available space is filled, old pages are removed as new pages are visited. You can opt for a new location for the temporary files folder, to view the folder or the view objects (program code).

The *History* section deals with the organisation of downloaded material. You can opt for a number of days to keep pages (1 to 999 days) or to *Clear* the history pages. A time setting of 30 days is a reasonable compromise.

The *Colors* button leads to a two-section pane. In the *Colors* section you can opt to use Windows colours, or to clear this option and specify background and foreground colours for yourself. The *Links* section allows you to specify colours for unused and used links and an optional *Hover* colour which will appear when the pointer is over the link. The colour choices for each are taken from a palette of 48 set colours, or you can create custom colours by selecting from a colour mixing display.

The *Font Setting* button can be clicked to select two main fonts. The main choice is of a font for proportional spacing, for which the default is *Times New Roman*. You can also select a fixed-spaced font, and for most users only *Courier New* is available. You can determine *Font size* from the five-size range of *Smallest* to *Largest*. You should not alter the *Character* set unless advised to do so.

Security: see the separate entry for **Security**.

Connection: The connection pane is concerned with how you first connect to the Internet, and has two sections, one for *Dialing* and the other for *Proxy Server* plus another for *Automatic Configuration* on a local network. The *Dialing* section is used if you connect by way of a modem connected to your computer, and you should have the box labelled *Connect to the Internet using a modem* ticked if you connect in this way. The alternative is to connect through a local area network. For either of these you can click the *Settings* button to establish (or check) the modem or LAN settings that are being used. In the modem settings you can opt to connect automatically to update *Channels*, to disconnect after an idle period whose time you can specify, and to perform system security checks before connecting. You can also specify how to re-dial an engaged number. The *Settings* button is not available if you connect through a LAN.

Programs: The *Programs* pane is concerned with programs that you use along with Internet Explorer. The *Messaging* section allows you to specify the programs used for Mail and News actions, and the default for each is, not surprisingly,

Microsoft Outlook Express, which replaces the older Microsoft Internet Mail and Microsoft Internet News. If you use other programs for Mail or News, you should specify them here by clicking on the arrowhead to see options. There is a line labelled *Internet Call*, but no default operating program is currently offered.

The *Personal Information* section contains *Calendar* and *Contact List*, with no default offered for *Calendar*. The only option for *Contact List* is *Address Book* unless you have other suitable programs running.

Advanced: This is a large set of option boxes divided into sets headed *Accessibility*, *Browsing*, *Multimedia*, *Security*, *Java*, *Printing*, *Searching*, *Toolbar* and *HTTP 1.1* settings

The Accessibility settings are:

Move system caret with focus/selection change and
Always expand alt text for images

The Browsing options are:

Notify when downloads complete
Disable script debugging
Show Channel bar at startup (if Active Desktop off)
Launch Channels in full-size window
Launch Browser in full-size window
Use AutoComplete
Show friendly URLs
Use smooth scrolling
Enable page transitions
Browse in a new process
Enable page hit counting
Enable scheduled subscription updates
Show Welcome message each time I log on
Show Internet Explorer on the Desktop (requires restart)
Underline links (always, never, or hover)

and the *What's This* help action can be used to provide details about the action each of these. The browser action is not impeded if none of these items is ticked, and the AutoComplete action is more often a nuisance than a help.

The Multimedia options are:

Show pictures
Play animations
Play videos
Play sound
Smart image dithering

and you can significantly increase the speed of browsing by keeping all of these options turned off. If you are interested mainly in textual content the absence of pictures is no handicap except where a picture is used to indicate a position to click. A small logo placeholder will appear in the position of each picture, and you can right-click this and select the *Show Picture* item.

The *Security* options are:

Enable Profile Assistant
PCT1.0
SSL 2.0
SSL 3.0
Delete saved pages when browser closed
Do not save encrypted pages to disk
Warn if form submit is redirected
Warn if changing between secure and insecure mode
Check for certificate revocation
Warn about invalid site certificates
Cookies (always accept, prompt, never accept)

Of these, *Enable Profile Assistant* deals with Web sites that read the information that is held in your *Profile* pages regarding how you want the (shared) computer configured when you are using it. Enabling the *Assistant* ensures that you have control over what information is released. If you

242

are working with a computer that is used by others you might want to tick the options regarding saved pages, since this will prevent others reading these items. You should certainly tick all of the other items in this set.

You will have to decide about **cookies** for yourself. A cookie is a file of information that resides on your hard drive and which is placed there by a Web site and which can be accessed by that site. If you refuse all cookies, some Web pages might not run. If you accept prompting you may waste time in clearing prompts. You might prefer to accept all cookies and to delete them, after each browser session, from the folder C:\windows\cookies. Many cookies are simple text files, such as a question that you have put to a search engine.

The other portions of the *Advanced* tab are shorter. The *Java* section allows you to enable the JIT Java console (requiring a restart), to enable the Java compiler, meaning that programs that use the Java language will be translated into code and run (just in time) when you click on the link that starts them. The other Java option is to keep a log of Java programs to aid trouble-shooting if problems arise as a result of running a Java program.

The *Printer* option is whether or not to print background colours and pictures. Enabling this option will add considerably to the time needed to print pages, and use a lot more of your costly coloured ink. The *Searching* option is *Autoscan common root domains*, and this is useful, because it will correct an entry that contains an incorrect domain (such as **com** instead of **ac**, for example). In this section also you can opt to search, prompt or not search for a similar address when you have typed an incorrect address.

The *Toolbar* options are to show fonts and to use small icons, and you will probably want to tick both. Finally, the

Windows 98 assistant

HTTP 1.1 option will be ticked for whatever case applies to you (lone user or network user).

Volume Control

General: The Volume Control is a display of a set of slider controls for use with a sound card when you are using Multimedia. The easiest way of using the *Volume Control* is to keep it as an icon on the Taskbar. Clicking this icon will bring up the volume control display. For some sound cards, a single click will bring up a simple volume control, and a double-click will bring up a sound mixer panel.

Place on Taskbar: Start Control Panel from Explorer or from Start — Settings, and click *Multimedia*. On the first tab, labelled *Audio*, click the selection box marked *Show Volume Control on Taskbar* so that the box is ticked.

Running: If the volume control icon (a loudspeaker shape) appears on the Taskbar at the right hand side, click on it. If you are not using the Volume Control on the Taskbar, click Start — Programs — Accessories — Multimedia — Volume Control.

Using: The simple Volume Control is a single slider control with a mute box. The more elaborate Volume Control is a mixer that displays slider controls for all the inputs and outputs that your sound card can deal with. A typical set is *Volume Control, Wave, MIDI, CD, Line in, Microphone* and *PC Speaker*. The *Volume Control* slider is a master control, and the settings of the others should be organised so that they all give about the same signal level, in or out, for a given setting of the master *Volume Control* slider. You can mute any of the sources, and if you are using the *Volume Control* for recording, you should mute all inputs except the one you want to use. Similarly, on replay, you should mute all outputs except the one you intend to use, which is likely to be *CD*. You can also change balance for stereo signals for each channel.

Options: The *Advanced* button will appear when you use Options — Advanced Controls. Clicking this button allows you to adjust *Bass* and *Treble* response. A *Bass* response setting higher than normal can be used partially to compensate for the deficiencies of small loudspeakers

Notes: If you often play audio CDs through the system you should place the *Volume Control* on the Taskbar.

Web pages

General: A Web page is a document that can contain text, images, sounds and hyperlinks. Web pages are written using a special form of text called *HTML*, meaning hypertext markup language, and the package called Front Page Express allows you to edit and create Web pages (click Page from the Edit menu of IE4). Creation of Web pages is not covered in this book.

Home page: The *Home Page* (or Start Page) is the page that appears when you start up Explorer. By default this is the *Microsoft Home Page*, and you can alter this to a blank page, or to a page you are currently viewing. Click View — Internet Options and in the Home Page section click *Use Current*, *Use Default* or *Use Blank*.

Viewing: A Web page will appear for viewing when it has downloaded. Some of the text may be visible before pictures or hyperlinks appear. When you type an address and press RETURN, or click a link, you will see the progress reports in the Status bar (which is why it should be turned on). The usual sequence is connecting, awaiting reply and downloading, and the screen will display the previous page until new material arrives.

Windows 98 assistant

You can also view offline. If you load several pages in sequence, you can then disconnect and view the text. Note that pictures are not retained for viewing. If you want to start IE4 offline, make sure that the File — Work Offline item is ticked when you close down.

Saving: You can save the text of the current page that you are viewing by clicking File — Save As, selecting a folder for the file, and typing a name (then click *Save*). If you want to save a picture, right-click the picture and use the *Save Target As* command, selecting a folder and filename as usual.

You can also copy text from a Web page into another document (**not** into another Web page). Select the text (use Edit — Select All if necessary) and click Edit — Copy. You can then past the text into another open document.

Adding to bars: You can add a Web address into various toolbars and lists for faster access. While you are viewing a page, click Favorites — Add to Favorites to add this page to the *Favorites* list (you can change its name). You can use the Favorites — Organise Favorites item to create new folders and to move or copy addresses into folders.

You can add a page to the Links bar by dragging the page icon (at the left hand side of the Address Bar) into the Links bar (or into the *Links* folder in the Favorites list). You can also drag a hyperlink in the current page to your Links bar. You can also drag a link from one place in the Links bar to another. When you drag a link, the pointer will change shape to show where a link can be inserted, which must be between other links or at either end of the bar.

Font size: Use the View — Fonts menu to select any of the five font sizes.

Copying and printing: Right-click over any selected item to get the *Copy, Select All, Print* menu.

Custom display: Use the View — Internet Options General page and click the buttons marked *Colors* or *Fonts*. The other buttons of *Accessibility* and *Languages* are more specialised.

What's This?

General: The *What's This* icon of a question mark is useful for getting more detailed information on portions of a panel, particularly if you want to know how to fill in a form.

Icon: When the question-mark icon appears on the right hand of the title bar of a window, or when the *Help* menu contains a *What's This* item, you can use this type of *Help*.

Method: Click on the icon or on the menu item. A question mark icon will appear on the pointer, and you can move the pointer to the part of the window that puzzles you and click there. After a short wait, a *Help* item will appear which gives specific guidance on that item.

Notes: *What's This* may be brief, but it allows you to query each part of an elaborate panel before you enter any information. For some topics, however, there may be no help or the help that appears may not be the correct item.

Window

General: A window can be maximised, filling the screen, or minimised, reduced to an icon on the Taskbar. Between these extremes, you can resize most windows by dragging their edges or corners, though a few, like Windows Calculator, cannot be resized. You can opt for using a specified window size when a program is started by way of a shortcut, see the entry for **Shortcuts**. Closing a window is equivalent to quitting a program.

Windows 98 assistant

Icons: Each window will normally contain a set of three icons at the top right hand corner of the window, and a Microsoft or other icon (menu icon) at the top left hand corner. The set of three icons will contain the cross icon which is used to close the window, and two of the three possible size icons of *minimise, normal* and *maximise*. The minimise icon will reduce the window to an icon and name on the Taskbar. The maximise icon will cause the window to take up all the useable screen area. The normal icon can be clicked to make the window resume the size that it had when last resized (not minimised nor maximised).

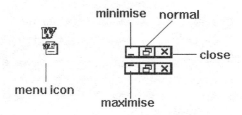

Menus: Clicking the Microsoft or other icon at the top left-hand corner of a window will bring up a menu of *Restore, Move, Size, Minimise, Maximise* and *Close*. Double-clicking the icon will close the window – this is an alternative to clicking on the cross icon.

Size: Drag any edge or corner of a window to alter the window size. Dragging a corner is preferable because it allows you to change both width and depth in one action. A few windows, such as Calculator, cannot be resized because they contain items, such as buttons, whose size is fixed.

Closing program: A program is closed when its window is closed, but you may prefer to close a program by using the *Exit* option in its *File* menu, or the equivalent. A few programs (such as communications programs) will not necessarily terminate when their window is closed. You will have to check for yourself if closing Explorer or Outlook Express will automatically disconnect you from the Internet.

Starting window size: Using Explorer, click on a shortcut to a program file and then on File — Properties. Click on the tab labelled *Shortcut*, and then click the arrowhead on the *Run* space. This offers the choice of *Normal Window*, *Maximized* or *Minimized*. Click your choice and then on the *OK* button.

Notes: The left-hand top corner icon can be clicked with either left or right-hand mouse button. The right-hand top corner icons can be clicked only with the left-hand mouse button.

- Remember that you can *Minimize All Windows* by clicking with the right-hand mouse button on a vacant part of the Taskbar and selecting this item.

Windows update

General: Windows Update can be used only if you have an Internet connection using Internet Explorer. It scans your system and lists the hardware and software you are using, and uses this list to find if any updated drivers or other software can be downloaded from the Web. Updates can be listed so that you can decide for yourself whether or not to use one. If you install an update, you can uninstall it later if you want. The content of Windows update is constantly changing, so that you should check for new updates at intervals.

Running: Click Start and then on Windows Update. When the site is connected, follow the instructions you see downloaded from the Update site.

WordPad

General: WordPad is the word processor for Windows 98, first introduced in Windows 95, that replaces the older *Write* used in Windows 3.1. The advantage of using WordPad is that its files are identical to those of Word 7, and the older Write files can be read. Some facilities of *Write* have not been retained, such as *Header and Footer* text, or a line-spacing option. For some purposes, such as preparation of books or articles, this makes WordPad less satisfactory than the older version, so that its main use is for reading, editing, or creating documents that are too long for Notepad. If you already use Word, then there is little point in retaining WordPad on the hard drive.

- The Windows 98 version supports files of Word 97, and also the Unicode text file and Rich Text Format (RTF) formats.

Opening: Start WordPad from Start — Programs — Accessories, assuming that the program has been placed in this menu when Windows 98 was installed. You can make a shortcut to WordPad in any part of the Start menu, or in any other folder, as you find convenient.

Screen: WordPad uses a screen appearance that is similar to Word 7, with a set of action icons on a *Toolbar*, font details on a *Formatting bar*, a *Ruler* and a *Status bar*. The *Toolbar*, *Format bar*, *Ruler* and *Status bar* can all be turned on or off using the *View* menu.

Page Setup: Before a document is printed (and preferably before it is typed) use File — Page Setup to define the paper size and other details. The size box contains the selection of paper and envelope sizes as follows:

A4	210×297 mm	A5	210×148 mm
#10 envelope	$4\frac{1}{8} \times 9\frac{1}{2}$	C5 envelope	162×229 mm

C6 envelope	114 × 162 mm	DL envelope	110 × 220 mm
Executive	7¼ × 9½ inch	Legal	8½ × 14 inch
Letter	8½ × 11 inch		

You can also opt for a User-defined size and then provide the dimensions for yourself.

You can also opt for Portrait (long side vertical) or Landscape (long side horizontal) paper orientation, and you can set the margins. The units of measurement are as defined in *Options*, see later. The default margins are 25 mm at left and right and also at top and bottom.

Options: Click View — Options for the option panel of six tabs labelled as *Options*, *Text*, *Rich Text*, *Word*, *Write* and *Embedded*. The *Options* tab can be clicked to allow you a choice of four measurement units, inches, centimetres, points or picas. The point is a unit of $^1/_{72}$ inch, and a pica is 12 points. You can also check a box for *Automatic word selection* which ensures that a selection action will not leave any word cut in two.

The other five tabs deal with the different forms of text files that WordPad can read, and in each panel you will find options for *Word Wrap* and for *Toolbars*. The *Word Wrap* options are *No wrap*, *Wrap to Window* and *Wrap to Ruler*, and the *Toolbars* options are *Toolbar*, *Format Bar*, *Ruler* and *Status Bar*. This allows you to determine how Wordpad will look when you are importing and editing these files. You might, for example, want to use plain text with no word wrap and all Toolbars off, but use Word-6 files with word wrap to *Ruler* and with all *Toolbars* on.

Formatting: The WordPad Format menu allows four choices, *Font*, *Bullet type*, *Paragraph* and *Tabs*. The *Font* choice covers all of the fonts that have been installed into your computer, but you should use only the TrueType fonts if you want to print your work. Bullets are large dots used to make a paragraph or line more prominent, and you can use the *Bullet type* item on the menu to convert an ordinary paragraph into one that starts with a bullet and is indented. There is no choice of bullet characters. The *Bullet* icon on the Toolbar is an alternative to the use of the menu, and you can remove a bullet by clicking again either on the icon or on the menu item.

The *Paragraph* menu item provides a panel on which you can select indentation for a paragraph in terms of *Left*, *Right* and *First Line*. You can indent a whole paragraph or have the first line with a larger indent or with a zero or smaller indent (a hanging indent). You can also choose the alignment for the paragraph as *Left*, *Center* or *Right*, but not, alas, for full alignment, which is much more desirable in printed documents.

The *Tabs* item allows you to specify a tab position by typing in the distance from the left margin and clicking on the *Set* button (or on the *Clear* button to clear a tab at that position). The faster alternative is to click on the ruler line so that a dotted vertical line appears. This can be dragged to wherever you want to set a tab, and such tabs can be removed by dragging them off the *Ruler* line. If you do not set any tabs, a set of default tabs, which cannot be removed, at ½ inch spacings will be used. These default tabs are indicated by small dots under the *Ruler*; the tabs that you set for yourself are indicates by larger square dots. When you set a tab by using the menu or the *Ruler* line, the default tabs to the left of your tab setting will be ignored, but the default tabs will continue to be used to the right of the last tab that you set for yourself. The menu action allows you to remove all of the tabs that you have set, using a *Clear All* button.

Insertions: You can use the Insert menu to insert *Date and Time* or *Object*. *Clicking Date and Time* will insert the current information into your WordPad document at the position of the cursor, and you can select from six date formats and two time formats. These are:

04/07/96	4/7/96	040796	04 July 1996
4 July 1996	09:49:43	9:49:43	

The first time format uses a 24-hour clock, the second uses PM to show times later than noon.

Object insertion covers the insertion of other text files, drawings and sounds, and the following description concentrates on insertion of a graphic to serve as an example. When you click on *Object* you will see a panel that allows you to choose *Create New* or *Create from File*. The *Create from New* item will allow you to run a program, in this example a Graphics program, to create the object so that it can be inserted. Using the *Create from File* option allows you to browse for a suitable graphics document file to use.

When you have found a file, you can click the box marked *Link* to link the file, or leave the box unticked to embed the file. When you opt to create a file, the program that you choose opens and you can make your drawing, but you should not use the File menu to close the file, because the File menu that you see is likely to be that of WordPad. When you use the *Create* option, you return to WordPad by clicking outside the file area, and the drawing or other object is embedded, not linked. If you want to link files, you have to create the file separately and save it before using WordPad to insert the object.

When an object is linked or embedded, you can use Edit — Properties from WordPad to see information about the object. For an embedded object, such as would be created using *Create from New*, the *Edit* panel has two tabs marked *General* and *View*. The *General* panel shows the *Type*, *Size* and *Location* of the object, with a button marked *Convert*

Windows 98 assistant

that is available if the object can be converted to another format. If, as is more usual, the object cannot be converted, the button is greyed out. The *View* panel has options *Display as Editable Information* and *Display as Icon*, with a button marked *Change Icon* that can be used if you opt for display as an icon. Icon display is more usual for sound objects, and the sound will be heard when you double-click the icon. For a graphics file, double-clicking the icon produces a view of the drawing. In this panel, there is also a *Scale* display, allowing you to change the percentage scaling for objects that allow this action. You can also opt for scaling *Relative to Original Size* if the object can be scaled.

There is a third tab for linked objects. This shows the file to which the links are attached, and a button marked *Change Source* which you can press to link in a different file. An *Update* section has options of *Automatically* (the default) or *Manually*, and there are buttons *for Open Source*, *Update Now* and *Break Links*. If the link has been updated previously, the *Last Update* information will appear.

- The *Edit* menu also contains a *Links* item when a linked image is selected, allowing you the same actions as are present in the third *Properties* tab.

The *Edit* menu also has another reference to an embedded or linked object. The item names the object, such as *Bitmap Image Object* or *Linked Bitmap Image Object*. In either case, selecting this item will provide the options of *Edit* or *Open*. For a linked object, either will start a graphics editor (Paint for a bitmap image) running, but for an embedded object, *Edit* will allow editing in the document and *Open* will start the creating program running. To leave an *Edit*, click outside the object space, but to leave the *Open* action you need to quit the program, such as Paint, from a File — Exit and Return to Document command.

Toolbar: The Toolbar of WordPad contains icons for *New*, *Open*, *Save*, *Print*, *Print Preview*, *Find*, *Cut*, *Copy*, *Paste*, *Undo* and *Time/Date insertion*. These provide faster alternatives for actions that are also catered for in the menus. You can switch the Toolbar off by using the *View* menu.

Send: The File — Send item will send a copy of the WordPad document by electronic mail, assuming that you have installed Microsoft Exchange. When you click on the *Send* item, the file is saved, and a Wizard takes over.

Notes: When you click on a text file, Notepad will automatically be used (see entry for **association**) but if the file is too large for Notepad to handle you will be offered the option of using WordPad.

If WordPad is almost all you need in the way of word processing, you should take a look at a more advanced version that is available under the name CwordPad. This is obtained on the Web site:

http://www.cetussoft.com/cwordpad.htm

This version contains a spelling checker and transforms WordPad into a much more useful editor for all but a few professional purposes.

Working offline

General: This option is offered in both versions of Explorer and also in Outlook Express. It allows you to work with these programs without being connected to the Internet. If you tick the Work Offline option before closing these programs they will open with this option active.

Switching: You can switch the option on or off by using the Work Offline item in the File menu.

Windows 98 assistant

Going online: In general, if you click a Web hyperlink in Explorer or use the Tools — Send & Receive item in Outlook Express you will see a popup panel giving you the option to remain offline or to connect.

Note: This allows you to compose or read mail and to read or print Web pages when offline.

Year 2000 ready

General: Modern PC computers use BIOS chips that will correctly set the date after December 31st, 1999, and deal with the leap year 2000. Modern software will also cope with the year change, and you can set Windows 98 to be ready for the change when you are using older software that stores dates in two-digit format.

Setting: Click Regional Settings in Control Panel, and click on the *Date* tab. Look at the entry under the label When a two digit year is entered, interpret as a year between. This determines how a date like **02** in a program will be interpreted, and the default is that it will be a year between 1930 and 2029. You can alter the ending year of the century as needed — remember that you are likely to be using a different version of Windows in 2029.

Note: This has no effect on software that uses dates in four-digit form, or which shows 21st century dates in a format such as '02.